CONTENT MARKETIN G ROI

HOW TO BUILD A MILLION DOLLAR DIGITAL MARKETING AGENCY AND ANALYZING THE RETURNS ON INVESTMENT IN CONTENT MARKETING EFFORTS.

I0446750

TABLE OF
CONTENTS

Definition of Content Marketing 2
Importance of ROI Analysis in Content Marketing 2
Purpose of this Guide 2
Chapter 1 Understanding Content Marketing................................2
Types of Content in Content Marketing 2
Goals and Objectives in Content Marketing.................................2
Chapter 2 Measuring Content Marketing ROI 2
Key Performance Indicators (KPIs) 2
Tools and Metrics for ROI Analysis..2
ROI Calculation Methods...2
Chapter 3..2
Factors Affecting Content Marketing ROI 2
Content Quality and Relevance 2
Target Audience and Persona 2
Distribution Channels,Timing and Consistency 2
Chapter 4..2
Case Studies and Successful Content Marketing ROI Examples.......2
Lessons Learned from Failed Attempts on Content Marketing 2
Chapter 5..2
Strategies for Improving Content Marketing ROI..........................2
Content Optimization and Audience 2
Engagement Strategies,A/B Testing and Iteration 2
Chapter 6 Challenges and Obstacles,Common Pitfalls in ROI
Analysis Dealing with Uncertainty...2
Chapter 7..2
Future Trends in Content Marketing ROI 2
Emerging Technologies and Data Privacy and Ethics....................2
CONCLUSION 2
Looking Ahead,Additional Resources Tools and Software for ROI
Analysis 2
INTRODUCTION TO CONTENTS MARKETING......................1

INTRODUCTIO
N TO

CONTENTS MARKETING

In the present quickly developing computerized scene, the idea of "Content Promoting return for money invested" has turned into a critical subject for organizations looking to flourish. This isn't a fantasy however a genuine story of development, change, and the strong soul of a showcasing group.

Meet Jennifer, a committed showcasing chief, driving a group in a moderate sized programming organization. They had been putting critical time and assets into content advertising endeavors, delivering blog entries, recordings, and virtual entertainment crusades, however estimating the genuine profit from the venture had forever been subtle.

Jennifer's group ended up at a junction. They realized they were creating significant substance, yet the central issue lingered: Were their endeavors really paying off? Still up in the air to find an answer, perceiving that showing unmistakable return for capital invested was fundamental for the organization's development.

Jennifer began by carrying out a hearty investigation framework to follow the exhibition of their substance. This was the most important move towards development, empowering them to gather information on site traffic, web-based entertainment commitment, and lead age. With this information, they could start to comprehend what bits of content were reverberating with their crowd and which were crashing and burning.

The group's change went past gathering information. Jennifer urged her group to consider some fresh possibilities and make content that wouldn't just draw in guests yet in addition convert them into clients. They started making top to bottom aides and digital books that offered veritable benefit to their crowd, exhibiting their mastery in the product business.

As they kept on enhancing, they embraced a multi-channel approach, guaranteeing their substance contacted the right crowd through different stages. They enhanced their site for web indexes and used email promoting to support leads. Web-based entertainment was utilized for broadcasting content as well as for taking part in discussions and building a local area around their image.

Versatility turned into a principal trait of Jennifer's group. Content showcasing is a speculation that expects time to yield results, and Jennifer figured out this. When confronted with variances in rush hour gridlock and lead age, the group stayed undaunted. Rather than overreacting, they examined the information, changed their systems, and persevered.

Jennifer's group ended up procuring their rewards for so much hard work. As their substance promoting endeavors developed, they saw a vertical pattern in site traffic, higher commitment via web-based entertainment, and a consistent expansion in leads. The return for money invested was turning out to be more obvious as time passed.

One of the most moving minutes for the group was the point at which a huge client credited their choice to buy the organization's product to a far reaching whitepaper the group had distributed. The association among content and income had never been more clear.

With these outcomes close by, Jennifer chose to impart their excursion to the organization's initiative. She introduced an extensive report showing how content promoting had straightforwardly added to income development. The imaginative procedures, change of their substance, and it were evident to relentless versatility.

The initiative was enlivened by the account of this promoting group. They perceived the force of content advertising and designated more assets to additional scale these endeavors. Jennifer's group was given the go-ahead to proceed with their inventive methodology, making a far reaching influence all through the association.

Before long, the organization's income kept on taking off. The genuine story of Jennifer and her group's endeavors filled in as a guide of motivation for different divisions, empowering them to take on a comparable information driven, imaginative, and strong way to deal with their work.

This rousing excursion of advancement, change, and flexibility displayed the substantial effect of content promoting on return on initial capital investment. Jennifer and her group showed that it's tied in with making content as well as about grasping your crowd, changing methodologies, and enduring through difficulties. This genuine example of overcoming adversity fills in as an update that with the right mentality and the assurance to improve, change, and endure, any organization can open the maximum capacity of content promoting and understand a striking profit from speculation.

Definition of Content Marketing

Content showcasing is a multi-layered procedure utilized by organizations and people to draw in, illuminate, and construct associations with their interest groups. Generally, it includes the creation, dispersion, and advancement of significant substance that resounds with a particular objective market. This promoting approach has acquired tremendous significance in the computerized age, offering a strong method for coming to and impacting likely clients.

At its center, content promoting is tied in with narrating. It's anything but a hard sell or an immediate notice; rather, it's an unobtrusive and instructive approach to passing on a message. This message could be anything from teaching a group of people about another item, sharing industry experiences, or basically engaging them with drawing stories. The goal is to offer some benefit, answer questions, and address the necessities of the crowd. Thus, happy advertising cultivates trust and reliability among clients.

Content showcasing takes many structures, from blog entries and articles to recordings, infographics, digital broadcasts, virtual entertainment updates, and that's only the tip of the iceberg. It's not restricted to a solitary medium; all things being equal, it use a blend of media to boost its compass and effect. This versatility is one of the qualities of content promoting, permitting it to line up with the inclinations of assorted crowds.

The essential objective of content showcasing is to draw in and hold a plainly characterized interest group. It's not only about drawing in countless guests or producing enormous traffic; all things being equal, it's tied in with drawing in the ideal individuals - the people who are truly keen on the substance and the items or administrations being advertised. This approach depends on the rule that by conveying significant substance, organizations can make a pool of connected and steadfast clients.

Content showcasing likewise assumes a huge part in building brand mindfulness. It is an essential device for making a brand more unmistakable and vital in the personalities of the crowd. Through reliable and top notch content, a brand can become related with mastery and authority in a specific field. For example, an organization that spends significant time in open air stuff might distribute articles on climbing tips, setting up camp aides, and abilities to survive. Over the long haul, users come to see the brand as a confided in hotspot for open air guidance and gear.

A basic part of content showcasing is the circulation and advancement of content. It is only the starting to Make amazing substance; arriving at the interest group should be actually dispersed. This frequently includes utilizing different channels, for example, web-based entertainment, email promoting, site improvement (Web optimization), and that's just the beginning. Without a very much arranged conveyance methodology, even the most uncommon substance might slip through the cracks.

Consolidating Website optimization procedures is essential in happy showcasing. It helps content position higher in web crawler results, making it more discoverable to those looking for pertinent data. By advancing substance for catchphrases and guaranteeing it is organized well for web indexes, content advertisers can increment natural traffic to their sites.

Commitment is one more basic part of content promotion. It's sufficiently not to make content and trust it reverberates with the crowd; association is critical. Remarks, preferences, offers, and conversations via virtual entertainment stages are indications of a connection with the crowd. Viable substance showcasing supports discourse and cooperation, encouraging a feeling of local area around the brand.

Content promoting is a drawn out system. There's no need to focus on prompt outcomes however about building connections over the long run. It requires tolerance and consistency. Brands may not see moment returns, but rather the interest in happy advertising frequently takes care of as supported client faithfulness and trust. Dissimilar to conventional promoting, which can be meddlesome, content showcasing regards the crowd's knowledge and inclinations.

One of the fundamental parts of content advertising is the estimation of its adequacy. Dissimilar to some customary showcasing systems that can be tried to gauge, content advertising gives more than adequate information to evaluate its effect. Investigation devices can follow different measurements, for example, site traffic, commitment rates, change rates, and that's only the tip of the iceberg. By examining this information, organizations can refine their substance advertising techniques for further developed results.

Content promoting isn't only for organizations; it's a significant apparatus for people and associations in different spaces. Experts like authors, specialists, artists, and non-benefits can utilize content promoting to feature their work, associate with their crowd, and accomplish their targets. It's a way to enhance one's message and contact a more extensive crowd.

In outline, content showcasing is a dynamic and key methodology that spotlights on making and sharing important substance to draw in, illuminate, and fabricate associations with an ideal interest group. It underlines narrating and expects to draw in and hold the right crowd, as opposed to an expansive one. Through appropriation, commitment, and estimation, content advertising assists organizations and people with accomplishing their objectives, from expanding brand attention to building enduring client connections. Its versatility and adaptability make it a flexible and fundamental promoting device in the computerized age.

Importance of ROI Analysis in Content Marketing

Content advertising has turned into a vital piece of the cutting edge business scene. Organizations are concentrating on making and dispersing content to connect with their interest group. Nonetheless, in this time of information driven direction, organizations should figure out the significance of Profit from Venture (return on initial capital investment) examination in satisfied promotion. This examination is a critical instrument that not just measures the progress of content showcasing endeavors yet in addition guides future techniques and guarantees a maintainable and beneficial methodology.

Content Showcasing in the Advanced Age

Content showcasing includes the creation and conveyance of important, pertinent, and reliable substance to draw in and hold a plainly characterized crowd. This content can take many structures, including blog entries, recordings, virtual entertainment posts, infographics, and that's only the tip of the iceberg. While content showcasing has demonstrated its adequacy in building brand mindfulness and driving client commitment, it's not safe to the examination of responsibility and execution estimation.

In a computerized age where buyers are besieged with data and decisions, organizations are frequently tested to demonstrate the worth of their substance showcasing endeavors. This is where return for money invested in investigation becomes possibly the most important factor.

Grasping return for capital invested in Satisfied Showcasing

Return on initial capital investment is a major business metric that assesses the monetary outcome of a venture comparative with its expense. In happy promoting, return on initial capital investment examination goes past following preferences, offers, and site traffic. It evaluates how actually happy adds to the association's objectives, like income age, client obtaining, and brand building.

The Significance of return for money invested Examination in Satisfied Promoting

Showing Substantial Outcomes:

Return for money invested investigation assists content advertisers with evaluating the results of their endeavors. It permits them to address questions, for example, "How much income did our new blog entry produce?" or on the other hand "What's the monetary effect of our virtual entertainment crusade? This information-driven strategy provides unmistakable evidence of content showcasing's impact on the main issue.

Enhancing Asset Distribution:

Compelling return for money invested examination permits organizations to proficiently distribute assets more. It distinguishes which sorts of content, dispersion channels, or missions convey the best return. By redistributing assets to high-return for capital invested systems, organizations can boost their showcasing ventures.

Refining Content System:

Content showcasing is a continuous interaction that requires nonstop improvement. Return for money invested examination recognizes which content performs well and which doesn't. Advertisers can utilize this data to refine their substance methodology, making content that resounds with the main interest group and drives transformations.

Estimating the Client Excursion:

Content showcasing frequently assumes a huge part in directing clients through the deals pipe. Return for capital invested examination gives bits of knowledge into how various bits of content impact likely clients at different phases of the purchasing venture. This understanding can be important for fitting substance to the necessities of each portion of the crowd.

Adjusting Advertising to Business Objectives:

By assessing the return for money invested in content promoting endeavors, organizations can guarantee that their advertising methodologies line up with their general business targets. This arrangement is fundamental for long haul achievement and benefit.

Challenges in return on initial capital investment Examination for Content Showcasing

While the advantages of return on initial capital investment examination

in satisfied promoting are obvious, a few provokes should be tended to:

Attribution Displaying:

Figuring out which explicit piece of content or touchpoint prompted a change can be complicated. Attribution demonstrating appoints credit precisely, however it's not generally clear, particularly in multi-touchpoint client ventures.

Long haul Effect:

Some satisfaction may not yield quick outcomes but rather can affect brand insight and client steadfastness. Catching this worth in return on initial capital investment examination can be challenging.

Information Quality:

The precision of return on initial capital investment examination relies upon the quality and consistency of information. Fragmented or off base information can prompt mistaken ends and poor direction.

Delicate Measurements:

Not all happy advertising objectives are effectively quantifiable. Measurements like brand mindfulness and thought administration, while urgent, are "delicate" and can be challenging to change over into substantial return for money invested figures.

Systems for Compelling return for money invested Examination in Happy Promoting

To address these difficulties, organizations can execute procedures for compelling return for money invested examination:

Clear Objective Setting:

Begin by characterizing clear and quantifiable objectives for your substance promoting efforts. These objectives ought to be lined up with more extensive business targets.

Following Transformations:

Carry out powerful transformation following to ascribe explicit activities to precisely satisfied pieces. This might include setting up occasion following on your site or utilizing advertising mechanization instruments.

Attribution Models:

Use multi-contact attribution models to comprehend the commitment of various substance pieces all through the client venture. Models like first-contact, last-contact, or direct attribution can give a more complete perspective on satisfied presentation.

Speculation Following:

Work out the absolute expense of content creation, conveyance, and advancement. Incorporate both immediate and circuitous expenses, like worker compensations and programming memberships.

Predictable Information Assortment:

Guarantee that information assortment is predictable and solid. Routinely review your investigation apparatuses and information sources to keep up with information quality.

Benchmarking:

Look at your return on initial capital investment information against industry benchmarks to acquire a feeling of where your presentation stands comparative with your companions.

Taking everything into account

Return for money invested examination in satisfied promotion is fundamental for estimating the adequacy of missions, improving asset designation, and adjusting showcasing endeavors to business objectives. While it accompanies its difficulties, organizations that put resources into precise and far reaching return for capital invested examination are better situated to flourish in the cutthroat universe of content advertising. As innovation proceeds to develop and information examination apparatuses become more refined, the capacity to break down and further develop content showcasing return on initial capital investment will be a vital consideration in making reasonable progress.

Purpose of this Guide

Content promoting is a strong system that has become progressively fundamental for organizations in the computerized age. It includes making and dispersing important, pertinent, and predictable substances to draw in and connect with a main interest group. The reason for this content advertising guide is to investigate the complexities of content promoting, from its definition and significance to the procedures and best practices that can assist organizations with accomplishing their objectives.

1. Meaning of Content Advertising

Content showcasing is the method involved with making and conveying superior grades, important substances to draw in, draw in, and hold an obviously characterized crowd. This content can take different structures, including blog entries, recordings, online entertainment refreshes, infographics, and that's just the beginning. The focal thought behind happy promotion is to give data, diversion, or arrangements that resonate with the interest group, eventually driving them to make wanted moves, like making a buy or buying into a pamphlet.

2. The Significance of Content Promoting

Content promoting has acquired huge unmistakable quality because of its various advantages for organizations. The following are a couple of key motivations behind why content showcasing is pivotal:

a. Building Brand Authority: Making savvy and definitive substance can situate a brand as an industry chief. At the point when organizations reliably give significant data, they assemble trust and validity among their crowd.

b. Expanding Perceivability: Very much upgraded content can assist a business with positioning higher in web crawler results, prompting expanded natural traffic. Besides, captivating substance shared via online entertainment can grow a brand's compass.

c. Client Commitment: Content advertising is an incredible method for interfacing with clients. Through blog remarks, online entertainment conversations, and email reactions, brands can major areas of strength for encourage their crowd.

d. Lead Age: Quality substance can go about as a lead magnet. By offering significant assets like digital books or online courses, organizations can catch potential clients' contact data and support them through the deals channel.

e. Savvy Showcasing: Contrasted with conventional promoting, content showcasing frequently gives a superior profit from venture. It may very well be financially savvy, particularly for private ventures.

3. Content Promoting Methodology

An effective substance promoting technique includes cautious preparation and execution. Here is a bit by bit manual for making a successful substance promoting plan:

a. Characterize Your Objectives: Begin by distinguishing what you need to accomplish with your substance showcasing endeavors. Shared objectives incorporate expanding site traffic, creating leads, and further developing brand mindfulness.

b. Figure out Your Crowd: To make content that reverberates, you should have a profound comprehension of your ideal interest group. Foster purchaser personas to direct your substance creation.

c. Pick the Right Satisfied Types: Select the substance that organizes that line up with your crowd's inclinations and your image's abilities. This could incorporate blog entries, recordings, webcasts, infographics, or a blend of these.

d. Foster a Substance Schedule: Consistency is key in satisfied advertising. Make a substance schedule that frames what content will be made and when it will be distributed.

e. Make Great Substance: Quality is principal. Your substance ought to be well-informed, enlightening, and locking in. It ought to offer some incentive to your crowd.

f. Upgrade for Search engine optimization: Guarantee your substance is advanced for web search tools by including significant catchphrases, meta labels, and excellent connections.

g. Advance Your Substance: Share your substance on different showcasing channels, including virtual entertainment, email, and industry discussions. Paid publicizing can likewise support perceivability.

h. Break down and Refine: Consistently audit your substance promoting endeavors by examining key execution pointers (KPIs). Utilize these experiences to refine your methodology and advance your substance.

4. Content Promoting Best Practices

To upgrade the viability of your substance promoting endeavors, think about these accepted procedures:

a. Consistency: Consistency in satisfied creation and dissemination is fundamental for building a group of people and keeping up with their advantage.

b. Narrating: Use narrating strategies to make your substance more interesting and locking in. Individuals recollect stories better than dry realities.

c. Visual Substance: Integrate visual components, like pictures and recordings, into your substance. Visual content will generally be more shared and engaging.

d. Intelligent Substance: Explore different avenues regarding intelligent substance like tests, surveys, and overviews to increment commitment.

e. Email Showcasing: Use email promoting to support leads and keep in touch with your crowd. Customize your messages for improved results.

f. Visitor Posting: Consider visitor posting on legitimate sites in your industry to contact a more extensive crowd and fabricate backlinks.

g. Virtual Entertainment Commitment: Draw in with your crowd via virtual entertainment stages, answer remarks, and effectively partake in discussions connected with your industry.

5. Estimating Achievement

To decide the progress of your substance advertising endeavors, you ought to screen and gauge different measurements, for example,

a. Site Traffic: Examine the quantity of guests to your site and how they connect with your substance.

b. Change Rates: Track the level of guests who make the ideal move, for example, pursuing a pamphlet or making a buy.

c. Web-based Entertainment Measurements: Assess likes, offers, remarks, and adherent development on your virtual entertainment channels.

d. Email Commitment: Measure open rates, navigate rates, and change rates for your email crusades.

e. Website optimization Execution: Screen your rankings for target catchphrases and the natural traffic driven by your substance.

f. Profit from Speculation (return for capital invested): Compute the income produced comparative with the expense of your substance promoting endeavors. Content promoting is a flexible and strong system for organizations to interface with their crowd, construct authority, and drive results. By following a clear cut methodology, making excellent substance, and sticking to best practices, organizations can bridle the capability of content promoting to accomplish their objectives and flourish in the serious computerized scene. Recollect that content showcasing is a drawn out venture, and persistence and determination are critical to receiving its full rewards.

Chapter 1 Understanding Content Marketing

Content showcasing is a strong and developing methodology that has changed the manner in which organizations draw in with their crowd, construct brand mindfulness, and drive client commitment. In this 800-word investigation, we will dig into the key ideas of content advertising, its importance in the advanced age, key procedures, and the effect it has on organizations.

Content Showcasing Characterized

Content showcasing is the essential creation and dispersion of important, pertinent, and steady happy to draw in and connect with a particular interest group. Dissimilar to customary publicizing, which clearly advances items or administrations, content advertising centers around conveying data and amusement that addresses the crowd's issues. It's tied in with offering some benefit first and laying out entrust with potential and existing clients.

Importance in the Computerized Age

In the age of the web, data is promptly accessible, and shoppers are immersed with a variety of choices. To hang out in this computerized whirlwind, organizations should offer something beyond items or administrations. They should give data and experiences that engage shoppers to go with informed choices.

Content promoting is instrumental in this unique circumstance. By conveying content that tends to shopper trouble spots, instructs them, and engages them, organizations can separate themselves and fabricate a reliable client base. It's at this point not just about selling; it's tied in with turning into a confided in a wellspring of data and an accomplice in the client's excursion.

Key Methodologies in Happy Showcasing

Grasping Your Crowd: The underpinning of viable substance showcasing is knowing your interest group. Who are they?What are their necessities, tendencies, and pain points?When you comprehend your crowd, you can make content that impacts them.

Quality Substance Creation: Content ought to be great, instructive, and locking in. This can take different structures, including blog entries, recordings, infographics, webcasts, and online entertainment posts. The key is to convey content that offers worth to the crowd.

Consistency: Consistency is fundamental. Consistently distributing content assists with keeping your crowd drawn in and informed. It likewise indicates to web crawlers that your website is dynamic and definitive.

Website improvement (Search engine optimization): To guarantee your substance arrives at your interest group, advancing it for web indexes is imperative. This includes utilizing significant catchphrases, meta portrayals, and upgrading your substance structure. Web optimization helps your substance rank higher in web search tool results pages.

Virtual Entertainment Advancement: Web-based entertainment stages are amazing assets for dispersing content. Sharing substance on stages like Facebook, Twitter, Instagram, and LinkedIn can assist you with contacting a more extensive crowd and encourage commitment.

Email Advertising: Email advertising permits you to send content straightforwardly to your endorsers. It's a powerful method for keeping your crowd educated and drawn in with your image.

Investigation and Estimation: To refine your substance promoting procedure, you really want to examine

21

its presentation. Use instruments like Google Examination to follow measurements, for example, site traffic, commitment, and transformation rates. This information can assist you with settling on information driven choices and change your substance methodology on a case by case basis.

Influence on Organizations

Content showcasing significantly affects organizations in different ways:

Expanded Brand Mindfulness: By reliably conveying important substance, organizations can construct areas of strength for a presence and increment brand mindfulness. After some time, individuals come to perceive and trust the brand.

Client Commitment: Drawing in satisfaction encourages a more profound association with the crowd. It supports likes, offers, and remarks, which can transform into significant communications and connections.

Further developed Search engine optimization: Great substance that is streamlined for web search tools can further develop a site's pursuit rankings. At the point when your substance positions higher, more individuals find your image.

Lead Age: Content can be utilized to catch leads. Offering important substances in return for contact data is a typical lead age procedure. This permits organizations to construct a rundown of possible clients.

Thought Administration: Giving definitive substance in your industry lays out your image as an idea chief. This raises your status according to your crowd and rivals.

Client Maintenance: Content showcasing isn't just about drawing in new clients. It's likewise a device for holding existing ones. By conveying important data and updates, organizations can keep clients drawn in and steadfast.

Savvy Promoting: Content showcasing frequently has a lower cost contrasted with conventional promoting. Making and circulating substances can be practical, particularly for private ventures.

Quantifiable Outcomes: With the utilization of investigation and estimation instruments, organizations can follow the presentation of their substance promoting endeavors. This takes into account information driven changes and upgrades.

All in all, happy advertising is a necessary piece of current promoting systems. It's tied in with offering some benefit, building trust, and sustaining associations with your crowd. With the right methodologies and a guarantee to quality, organizations can outfit the force of content showcasing to accomplish their objectives, whether that is expanding brand mindfulness, drawing in clients, or driving deals. A dynamic and developing field keeps on forming the manner in which organizations associate with their crowd in the computerized age.

Types of Content in Content Marketing

Content promoting is a strong and fundamental technique for organizations in the computerized age. It includes making and circulating significant and important substances to draw in and connect with an ideal interest group.

The outcome of content showcasing relies on the different kinds of content that can be used to interface with purchasers and accomplish advertising targets. In this article, we'll investigate a complete outline of the kinds of content in satisfied promotion, featuring their qualities and the upper hands they offer.

Blog Entries:

Blog entries are a central part of content promotion. They are commonly useful, instructive, or engaging articles distributed on an organization's site.

Blog entries can address many points, making them flexible for various advertising objectives. They are important for Search engine optimization, driving natural traffic, and laying out thought administration.

Infographics:

Infographics are outwardly engaging portrayals of data or information. They are intended to improve on complex ideas and information into straightforward illustrations. Infographics are exceptionally shareable via web-based entertainment, making them a powerful method for connecting with crowds.

Videos:

Video content has seen dangerous development as of late. It incorporates many configurations, like item shows, instructional exercises, meetings, and activities. Video content is connected with and powerful in passing on messages, and it is leaned toward on stages like YouTube, Instagram, and TikTok.

Podcasts:

Digital broadcasts are sound accounts that can be consumed in a hurry. They offer a helpful method for interfacing with a group of people, particularly while examining inside and out or specialty points. Web recordings can be an important expansion to content promoting techniques, taking care of hear-able students.

Virtual Entertainment Posts:

Content showcasing via virtual entertainment stages includes a blend of text, pictures, recordings, and intelligent substance. Virtual entertainment presents are planned to draw in and collaborate with devotees, advancing brand mindfulness and directing people to sites.

Digital books and Whitepapers:

Digital books and whitepapers are long-structured composed content that dive profoundly into a particular topic. They are generally presented as downloadable assets in return for contact data. These substance types are great for lead age and laying out power.

Contextual investigations:

Contextual investigations give true instances of how an item or administration tackled an issue or conveyed esteem. They are powerful for exhibiting validity and building entrust with likely clients.

Email Showcasing:

Email promoting is a type of content showcasing that includes sending fitted substances straightforwardly to supporters' inboxes. This can incorporate bulletins, special offers, instructive substance, from there, the sky's the limit. Email advertising sustains leads and holds clients.

Client Created Content:

Client created content will be content made by clients or clients of an item or administration. It incorporates audits, tributes, and online entertainment posts that highlight your items. This sort of satisfaction adds vagueness and trust to your image.

Intuitive Substance:

Intuitive substance draws in clients effectively, for example, tests, surveys, and adding machines. It's a compelling method for gathering information, giving customized encounters, and encouraging client commitment.

Webinars:

Online classes are live or pre-recorded web-based workshops that give top to bottom data on a specific subject. They are fantastic for instructing and drawing in an ideal interest group.

Live Streaming:

Live gushing on stages like Facebook Live, Instagram Live, and Jerk offers continuous communication with a group of people. It's an amazing decision for item dispatches, interactive discussions, and in the background content.

Visual Substance:

Visual substance incorporates pictures, GIFs, and images. It's indispensable for narrating and catching the crowd's consideration via virtual entertainment stages.

Evergreen Substance:

Evergreen substance isn't time-touchy and stays important over a significant stretch. It can keep on driving traffic and create leads for quite a long time.

Miniature Minutes Content:

Miniature minutes content takes care of the prompt necessities and interests of clients. It gives fast, enlightening responses and is appropriate for versatile clients.

Long-Structure Content:

Long-structure content, for example, inside and out articles or guides, can lay out skill and authority regarding a matter. It's great for Website design enhancement and building an unwavering readership.

Intuitive Guides and Instruments:

For organizations in the movement, land, or instructive areas, intuitive guides and devices are significant. They can assist clients with pursuing informed choices and make a paramount encounter.

Client Tributes and Surveys:

Sharing genuine client tributes and audits on your site or web-based entertainment assembles trust and social confirmation.

Item Demos and Instructional exercises:

Giving nitty gritty item showings and instructional exercises assists clients with understanding your items better and urges them to make informed buys.

Stories and Microblogging:

Stages like Instagram and Snapchat offer highlights for sharing stories, which are impermanent and drawing in happy pieces that vanish after a set time. They are incredible for sharing in the background impressions and constant updates.

All in all, the universe of content showcasing is rich and different, offering a large number of content sorts to suit different promoting objectives and ideal interest groups.

The way to progress is understanding your crowd, making content that addresses their necessities and interests, and utilizing the right blend of content kinds to accomplish your promoting targets. Whether you're planning to assemble brand mindfulness, produce leads, or sustain client connections, the right satisfaction is your most powerful apparatus in accomplishing your objectives.

Goals and Objectives in Content Marketing

Content showcasing is an essential part of any fruitful computerized procedure. An essential methodology centers around making and conveying important, pertinent, and predictable substance to draw in and connect with an interest group. To capitalize on your substance advertising endeavors, defining clear and feasible objectives and objectives is fundamental. In this 800-word investigation, we'll dive into the meaning of defining objectives and targets in satisfied advertising and how it can drive your prosperity.

The Significance of Objectives and Targets

Objectives and targets are the directing stars in satisfied promotion. They give a guide to your endeavors, assisting you with keeping focused and measuring your advancement. Here is the explanation they are so critical:

1. Bearing and Concentration: Objectives and targets provide your substance promoting with an internal compass. They characterize what you need to accomplish, permitting you to zero in on exercises that straightforwardly add to your objectives.

2. Estimating Achievement: Setting clear goals makes it simpler to quantify the progress of your substance promoting endeavors. It assists you with recognizing what's working and what needs improvement.

3. Accountability: Objectives and goals make a feeling of responsibility inside your group. At the point when everybody understands what they are really going after, they can more readily adjust their endeavors.

4. Adaptability: As you survey your substance advertising endeavors against your objectives, you can adjust and refine your methodology depending on the situation. This adaptability is essential in the always developing advanced scene.

5. Asset Designation: Having characterized objectives assists you with allocating your assets all the more proficiently. You can contribute time, cash, and labor supply where it will have the most effect.

Laying out Shrewd Objectives

While defining objectives and goals for your substance promotion, the Savvy system is an important device.Clever addresses Unequivocal, Quantifiable, Attainable, Relevant, and Time-bound.How about we separate these parts:

1. Specific: Your objectives ought to be clear and distinct. Instead of saying, "Additional site traffic," you could decide, "Augmentation regular site traffic by 20%."

2. Measurable: Your goals should be quantifiable. Use measurements like traffic, commitment, transformations, or income to gauge progress.

3. Achievable: Your objectives ought to be sensible and achievable. Stretch objectives are perfect for inspiration, yet they ought to in any case be reachable.

4. Relevant: Guarantee that your objectives line up with your general business goals and the necessities and inclinations of your interest group.

5. Time-bound: Set a time span for accomplishing your objectives. For example, "Increment virtual entertainment supporters by 15% in a half year."

Kinds of Objectives and Targets

In satisfied promotion, there are different sorts of objectives and targets you can set, contingent upon your business and showcasing methodology. Here are a few normal models:

1. Awareness: In the event that you're simply beginning or have to grow your range, your objective may be to increment brand mindfulness. Goals could incorporate developing your online entertainment devotees or expanding site traffic.

2. Engagement: To encourage a more drawn in crowd, you could set goals like expanding the typical time spent on your site or the quantity of remarks and offers on your substance.

3. Lead Age: Assuming your point is to catch leads for your deals channel, you can define objectives connected with the quantity of leads produced, the transformation rate, or the development of your email list.

4. Conversions: At last, most organizations need to drive transformations. Objectives connected with this could be expanding item deals, recruits, or other explicit transformation activities.

5. Client Maintenance: Content promoting isn't just about securing new clients yet additionally holding existing ones. Targets could incorporate diminishing beat rate or expanding client lifetime esteem.

6. Thought Administration: At times, you could mean to lay out your image as an idea chief in your industry. Objectives could connect with the quantity of visitor posts in definitive distributions or talking commitment.

Adjusting Content to Objectives

Whenever you've put forth your objectives and goals, it's pivotal to guarantee that your substance lines up with them. Your substance ought to fill a need, and each piece ought to add to accomplishing your objectives. This is the method for getting it going:

1. Crowd Investigation: Comprehend your interest group's necessities, trouble spots, and inclinations. Tailor your substance to address these elements and resound with your crowd.

2. Content Sorts: Various sorts of content are appropriate for various objectives. For example, blog entries can assist with Search engine optimization and site traffic, while online classes may be more successful for lead age.

3. Content Dissemination: The channels you use to disperse your substance ought to line up with your objectives. Assuming your objective is brand mindfulness, web-based entertainment stages may be your concentration. For lead age, email promoting and greeting pages could be more significant.

4. Source of inspiration (CTA): Your substance ought to direct your crowd towards making the ideal move. Whether it's pursuing a bulletin, making a buy, or sharing a post, the CTA ought to be clear and convincing.

Estimating and Changing

Putting forth objectives and making content to accomplish them is only the start. Standard estimation and change are fundamental.The following are a couple of focal issues to consider:

1. Metrics: Utilize the measurements that are generally pertinent to your goals. This could incorporate site examination, virtual entertainment bits of knowledge, email open and navigate rates, or transformation information.

2. A/B Testing: Try different things with various substance ways to deal with and see what works best. A/B testing can assist you with refining your technique and further develop results.

3. Analysis: Routinely break down your substance execution. Recognize patterns, examples, and regions where you're missing the mark regarding your objectives.

4. Adaptation: In view of your examination, adjust your substance technique. Assuming that specific substance types or channels are reliably failing to meet expectations, consider redistributing assets.

5. Collaboration: Guarantee that your promoting and content groups work together really. They ought to share bits of knowledge and work together to improve content for accomplishing objectives.

Chapter 2
Measuring Content Marketing ROI

In the present computerized scene, content promoting has arisen as a strong methodology for organizations to associate with their crowds, fabricate brand mindfulness, and drive commitment. However, with the rising emphasis on showcasing responsibility, estimating the profit from speculation (return for money invested) of content promoting has turned into a central test. In this 800-word investigation, we dive into the complexities of estimating content showcasing return for capital invested, revealing insight into the basic measurements and best practices that can assist associations with opening the genuine worth of their substance endeavors.

Characterizing Content Advertising return for money invested

Content advertising return for money invested, in its least difficult structure, is the proportion of the additions from content promoting endeavors to the expenses brought about. This proportion can be addressed as:

return for money invested = (Net Increase from Content Advertising - Cost of Content Promoting)/Cost of Content Showcasing

To quantify it successfully, organizations need to decide both the net addition and the expenses. The net increase can be a moving measurement to evaluate straightforwardly, as happy showcasing frequently serves long haul goals like brand building, client trust, and thought initiative. Subsequently, it is fundamental to investigate the horde of measurements that by implication add to this net increase.

Distinguishing Key Measurements

Understanding substance promoting return for money invested begins with recognizing the right measurements to follow. Here are probably the most basic measurements:

a. Traffic and Commitment: One of the underlying signs of content advertising achievement is an expansion in site traffic. Google Investigation and other web examination instruments can give information on interesting guests, site visits, bob rates, and meeting spans. Commitment measurements, like social offers, remarks, and likes, are additionally significant marks of the substance's adequacy.

b. Lead Age: Content promoting frequently centers around catching leads. Estimating the quantity of leads produced through happiness is vital. Track the transformation rate from content to leads, and evaluate the nature of those leads.

c. Deals and Transformations: Eventually, the objective of most satisfied showcasing endeavors is to drive deals and transformations. Associate substance commitment to deals by dissecting transformation rates, deals credited to explicit substance pieces, and the client venture through the deals channel.

d. Brand Mindfulness: It is more subjective however similarly essential to Gauge brand mindfulness. Reviews, social tuning in, and opinion examination devices can give bits of knowledge into how content effects brand discernment and acknowledgment.

e. Client Maintenance: Content can be a useful asset for holding existing clients. Dissect the effect of content on client reliability, rehash buys, and stir rates.

Computing Expenses

To compute content showcasing costs, think about both immediate and circuitous costs. Direct expenses incorporate substance creation, dissemination, and advancement costs. Aberrant expenses incorporate compensations and above connected with content advertising. Catching the full extent of consumptions for a precise return for money invested assessment is significant.

Content Attribution Models

Ascribing content to changes can be mind boggling. Content frequently assumes a part at different phases of the client venture. Different attribution models, like first-contact, last-contact, and multi-contact attribution, can assist in designating with crediting to the substance pieces that affected changes.

Putting forth Clear Objectives

To quantify content advertising return on initial capital investment actually, organizations should set clear, explicit objectives. Objectives ought to be Brilliant - Explicit, Quantifiable, Reachable, Applicable, and Time-bound. Each satisfied piece ought to line up with at least one of these objectives, making it more straightforward to follow achievement.

Following Client Lifetime Worth

Estimating the prompt effect of content is fundamental, yet surveying its drawn out effects is similarly significant. Client Lifetime Worth (CLV) thinks about the worth of a client over their whole relationship with a business. Content can add to higher CLV by cultivating client faithfulness and rehash buys.

A/B Testing

A/B testing includes making at least two renditions of content and evaluating which one performs better. This approach gives information driven bits of knowledge into what resounds with the crowd and can work on a happy return for money invested over the long run.

Content Inspecting

Consistently evaluating your substance can help distinguish failing to meet expectations. By reusing, refreshing, or dispensing with inadequate substance, organizations can amplify return for money invested.

Benchmarking

Contrasting your substance showcasing return for money invested with industry benchmarks can give setting to your exhibition. Understanding how your outcomes stack facing contenders can direct your substance system.

Information Examination Devices

Use information examination devices and client relationship the executives (CRM) programming to gather and break down information successfully. Mechanization and information perception instruments can assist with smoothing out the cycle and give noteworthy experiences.

Attribution to Miniature and Full scale Changes

Not all satisfied fills a similar need. Think about both miniature and full scale changes in your return for capital invested estimation. Miniature changes, similar to email recruits, can add to large scale transformations like deals after some time.

Client Criticism

Client criticism, through studies or audits, can give significant subjective information on the effect of content showcasing. It can uncover client feelings, trouble spots, and regions where content has affected their choices.

return for money invested as a Drawn out Game

Content advertising return on initial capital investment frequently unfurls over a drawn out period. While momentary additions are significant, organizations ought to zero in on

37

building maintainable, long haul esteem through their substance endeavors.

Normal Announcing and Changes

Consistently evaluate and write about a satisfied showcasing return for money invested. Utilize the information to make informed changes in accordance with your substance procedure. Adaptability and variation are essential for improving substance showcasing return on initial capital investment.

All in all, estimating content promoting return for capital invested is a diverse undertaking that expects organizations to characterize clear objectives, track a scope of measurements, and designate expenses precisely. While return on initial capital investment may not generally manifest right away, satisfied promoting is a venture that can yield significant returns over the long haul.

Key Performance Indicators (KPIs)

Key Execution Pointers (KPIs) are fundamental measurements that associations use to assess their advancement towards explicit objectives and goals. These quantifiable estimations give important experiences into an organization's exhibition, assisting the executives with pursuing informed choices, screen progress, and streamline techniques. In this article, we will dive into the meaning of KPIs, how to characterize and quantify them, and a few normal models across different enterprises.

Grasping the Significance of KPIs

KPIs are the compass of an association, directing it toward progress. They serve a few basic capabilities:

Objective Arrangement: KPIs line up with the association's targets and assist with guaranteeing that all endeavors are coordinated towards accomplishing these objectives. They make a way and keep groups on target.

Execution Assessment: KPIs consider consistent appraisal of an association's exhibition. They give a depiction of how well the organization is doing and in the event that it is drawing nearer to its goals or digressing from them.

Decision-Making: KPIs empower information driven navigation. They offer a quantitative reason for recognizing issues, figuring out patterns, and making changes in accordance with techniques and tasks.

Communication: KPIs work with correspondence inside an association. They pass fundamental data on to different partners, assisting everybody with understanding the organization's exhibition and regions that require consideration.

Accountability: KPIs consider people and groups responsible for their parts in accomplishing authoritative targets. At the point when there are quantifiable focuses on, clear is liable for explicit results.

Characterizing and Estimating KPIs

Characterizing KPIs is a pivotal step, and it ought to be done insightfully.

Here is an interaction for setting and estimating KPIs:

Distinguish Objectives: Begin by plainly characterizing the association's objectives.What do you have to achieve? These can be monetary, functional, or vital goals.

Evaluate Objectives: Make these objectives quantifiable. For instance, on the off chance that you want to increment income, determine by which rate or sum.

Select KPIs: Pick KPIs that straightforwardly connect with your objectives. For income development, KPIs could incorporate deals income, client procurement cost, or client lifetime esteem.

Set Targets: Lay out unambiguous focuses for each KPI. These objectives ought to be sensible, feasible, and time-bound. For example, expanding income by 10% throughout the following quarter.

Information Assortment: Assemble pertinent information to quantify the chosen KPIs. This information might come from different sources, for example, deals reports, client criticism, or site investigation.

Ordinary Observing: Constantly track the KPIs to check whether you're on target to meet your objectives. Normal checking guarantees early location of issues and gives the open door to convenient changes.

Examination and Activity: At the point when KPIs show deviations from targets, break down the information and make proper moves. For example, assuming deals income is beneath the objective, you could change promoting procedures or send off new items.

Normal KPIs Across Enterprises

KPIs are adaptable and can be applied across different enterprises. Here are a few instances of normal KPIs in various areas:

1. Retail:
Deals per square foot: Measures the effectiveness of retail space use.
Stock turnover rate: Demonstrates how rapidly stock is sold.
2. Data Innovation:
Uptime and margin time: Measures framework accessibility and unwavering quality.
Bug goal time: Assesses the proficiency of the turn of events and backing groups.
3. Healthcare:
Patient fulfillment score: Measures the nature of patient consideration.
Normal length of stay: Demonstrates medical clinic proficiency.
4. Finance:
Profit from Venture (return on initial capital investment): Measures the productivity of ventures.
Resource turnover proportion: Assesses how productively resources are utilized to create income.
5. Manufacturing:
By and large Gear Adequacy (OEE): Measures the productivity of creation processes.
Deformity rate: Assesses item quality.
6. Marketing:
Change rate: Measures the adequacy of advertising efforts.
Cost per securing (CPA): Assesses the productivity of client procurement methodologies.
These models show the way that KPIs can be customized to explicit enterprises and objectives. Picking the right KPIs and observing them reliably are imperative strides for any association.
The Development of KPIs

Lately, KPIs have developed because of progressions in innovation and changes in strategic policies. Conventional KPIs were many times monetary in nature, zeroing in on income, benefit, and cost measurements. Be that as it may, present day KPIs additionally consider non-monetary factors like consumer loyalty, representative commitment, and ecological effect.

In addition, with the approach of huge information and examination, associations can now tackle more mind boggling KPIs. Prescient KPIs, for instance, utilize authentic information to estimate future execution. These experiences can direct essential choices with a drawn out point of view.

All in all, Key Presentation Pointers (KPIs) are key apparatuses for associations to quantify progress, assess execution, and drive direction. When appropriately characterized and checked, KPIs empower organizations to keep on track, adjust endeavors, and constantly adjust to a powerful business climate. As innovation keeps on advancing, KPIs will probably turn out to be significantly more complex, offering further experiences into hierarchical execution.

Tools and Metrics for ROI Analysis

Profit from Speculation (return on initial capital investment) is an essential measurement for assessing the viability and benefit of different business drives, tasks, or ventures. In the present information driven business climate, associations depend on a large number of devices and measurements to successfully perform return on initial capital investment examination. This examination helps in settling on informed choices, apportioning assets effectively, and amplifying benefits. How about we investigate a portion of the fundamental instruments and measurements utilized for return on initial capital investment examination:

Apparatuses for return for capital invested Examination:

Bookkeeping sheet Programming (e.g., Microsoft Succeed): Accounting sheets are the most well-known and flexible devices for return for money invested investigation. They empower organizations to make monetary models, perform computations, and picture information in an organized way.

Monetary Demonstrating Programming: Particular programming like Quantrix, Palisade's @RISK, and Prophet Hyperion takes into account more complicated monetary displays, integrating different situations and awarenesses.

Project The executives Programming: Devices like Microsoft Venture or Trello assist in following projecting expenses and timetables, which are significant for return for capital invested examination, particularly in project-based organizations.

Bookkeeping Programming: Stages, for example, QuickBooks or Xero can give exact monetary information to investigating return for capital invested, as they oversee pay, costs, and resources proficiently.

Client Relationship The executives (CRM) Programming: CRM devices like Salesforce or HubSpot help in following client securing costs, client lifetime esteem, and the return for capital invested of showcasing efforts.

Measurements for return for capital invested Investigation:

Profit from Venture (return for money invested): return for money invested is the most crucial measurement in return for capital invested examination. It is determined as (Net Benefit/Cost of Venture) * 100. A positive return for money invested demonstrates productive speculation.

Recompense Period: This measurement shows the time it takes for a venture to produce an adequate number of profits to recuperate the underlying expense. More limited compensation periods are for the most part liked.

Net Present Worth (NPV): NPV ascertains the current worth of future incomes, limited to the present. A positive NPV shows beneficial speculation.

Inside Pace of Return (IRR): IRR is the rebate rate that makes the NPV of a venture equivalent to nothing. Higher IRR values are for the most part more attractive.

Equal the initial investment Point: This measurement decides when the venture or speculation will begin producing a benefit and takes care of its underlying expenses.

Profit from Promoting Speculation (ROMI): ROMI assesses the return for money invested of showcasing endeavors by contrasting the expense of advertising efforts with the income produced.

Client Lifetime Worth (CLV): CLV measures the projected income a business can anticipate from a client all through their relationship. It helps in surveying the drawn out benefit of getting and holding clients.

Money saving advantage Investigation (CBA): CBA looks at the expenses of a task or speculation to the normal advantages, considering both monetary and non-monetary variables.

Risk Appraisal Measurements: These measurements assess the degree of hazard related with a venture, like awareness investigation, situation examination, or Monte Carlo recreations.

Social Profit from Speculation (SROI): SROI evaluates the more extensive social and ecological effect of ventures, including factors like manageability and local area prosperity.

Monetary Worth Added (EVA): EVA estimates the monetary presentation of an organization by deducting the expense of capital from its net working benefit.

Client Procurement Cost (CAC): CAC works out the costs caused to gain another client, giving bits of knowledge into the effectiveness of advertising and deals endeavors.

Consistency standard: This measurement evaluates the level of clients who keep on working with an organization over the long haul, influencing the drawn out return for capital invested of client procurement.

Taking everything into account, return for capital invested examination is an irreplaceable cycle for associations intending to go with sound monetary choices and boost their benefit. The devices and measurements referenced above are fundamental in directing careful return for money invested examination. While the apparatuses give the resources to accumulate and control information, the measurements offer the quantitative and subjective experiences important to pursue informed choices. A top notch return on initial capital investment investigation enables organizations to designate assets carefully, focus on speculations, and at last drive reasonable development.

ROI Calculation Methods

Profit from Speculation (return on initial capital investment) is a basic monetary metric that assists organizations with evaluating the productivity and proficiency of different ventures. It's a proportion of the return or gain on a speculation comparative with its expense. Return on initial capital investment computation strategies are fundamental devices for chiefs, assisting them with assessing the practicality of undertakings, drives, or ventures. In this article, we'll investigate different return for money invested estimation techniques, their benefits, and their impediments.

Essential return on initial capital investment Estimation:

The most direct return for capital invested estimation strategy is the essential equation:

$$ROI = \frac{(InvestmentCost)}{(NetGainorLoss)} \times 100$$

This technique gives a basic method for surveying the productivity of a venture. It's not difficult to work out and comprehend, making it generally utilized in different fields. Nonetheless, it tends to be excessively shortsighted and may not represent the time worth of cash or the term of the speculation.

Net Present Worth (NPV):

NPV adapts to the time worth of cash by limiting future incomes to their current worth. The recipe for NPV is:

$$NPV = \sum \left(\frac{CF}{(1+r)t} \right) C$$

Where:

CF addresses the income for every period.

r is the markdown rate.

t is the time span.

C is the underlying speculation cost.

NPV is broadly utilized in monetary examination, assisting chiefs with representing the open door cost of capital and giving a more precise image of a speculation's possible return.

Inner Pace of Return (IRR):

IRR is the markdown rate that makes the net present worth of a speculation equivalent to nothing. It's utilized to assess the likely profit from a speculation in light of the normal incomes and beginning venture. The recipe for IRR is normally tackled iteratively utilizing monetary programming or number crunchers.

IRR can be more perplexing to compute contrasted with fundamental return for capital invested, yet it offers a more modern examination that considers the time worth of cash. It's particularly helpful for contrasting numerous speculation choices.

Restitution Period:

The restitution time frame is the time it takes to recuperate the underlying speculation. It's determined as follows:

(AnnualCashInflows)
PaybackPeriod=

_____
(InitialInvestment)

The compensation time frame is a basic metric that is straightforward. More limited recompense periods are by and large linked, as they show quicker profits from ventures. Nonetheless, this technique doesn't think about incomes past the recompense period, possibly neglecting long haul productivity.

Productivity List (PI):

The benefit file assesses the productivity of a speculation by looking at the current worth of future incomes to the underlying venture. The equation is:

(InitialInvestment)
PI=   _____
(PVofFutureCashFlows)

A PI more noteworthy than 1 shows a possibly beneficial speculation. This strategy represents the time worth of cash and gives an unmistakable proportion of relative benefit.

Profit from Advertising Speculation (ROMI):

ROMI is explicitly used to survey the viability of advertising efforts. It considers not just the income produced by a promoting drive yet additionally the expense of that drive. The equation is:

$$ROMI = \frac{(MarketingCosts)}{(NetMarketingContribution)} \times 100$$

ROMI permits advertisers to figure out which missions or channels convey the best profit from speculation, helping with the allotment of assets for future promoting endeavors.

Social Profit from Speculation (SROI):

SROI is a strategy used to assess the social and ecological effect of speculations. It factors in monetary returns as well as friendly and natural results. Working out SROI can be perplexing, as it includes appointing values to non-monetary effects.

Every one of these return for capital invested estimation strategies has its assets and constraints. The decision of strategy relies upon the particular idea of the speculation or undertaking being surveyed. Essential return on initial capital investment is straightforward and fast however may ignore significant monetary contemplations. Further developed techniques like NPV and IRR offer a more extensive examination however can be more perplexing to apply. The restitution time frame gives a fast evaluation of when a speculation will earn back the original investment, however it doesn't think about long haul returns. Benefit File, ROMI, and SROI take care of explicit requirements in money, advertising, and social effect assessment.

All in all, return for money invested estimation techniques are essential apparatuses for surveying the feasibility of speculations and undertakings. Chiefs should pick the most suitable strategy in light of the particular setting and goals of the examination. A careful comprehension of these techniques can enable organizations and associations to go with educated and vital venture choices, at last driving monetary achievement and practical development.

Chapter 3
Factors Affecting Content Marketing ROI

Top notch Content: The foundation of content promoting achievement is excellent substance. Well-informed, instructive, and connecting with content draws in your main interest group as well as keeps them locked in. Quality substance lays out your clout in your specialty and supports sharing and backlinks, all of which add to a higher return for capital invested.

Content Significance: Significance is critical. On the off chance that your substance doesn't reverberate with your interest group's necessities, interests, and trouble spots, it won't yield the normal outcomes. Content should resolve explicit issues or questions, lining up with the client venture at different stages.

Compelling Catchphrase Technique: Content promoting frequently meets with Website design enhancement (Site improvement). A very much arranged catchphrase procedure guarantees that your substance positions well in query items, expanding its perceivability. This, thus, prompts more natural traffic and higher return on initial capital investment.

Consistency: Consistency in happy creation and distributing is fundamental. An irregular methodology can prompt irregularity in rush hour gridlock and commitment. Ordinary substance refreshes and a substance schedule can keep up with crowd interest and result in an additional steady return for money invested.

Content Dispersion Channels: The decision of dissemination channels significantly affects content showcasing return for money invested. Contingent upon your crowd and objectives, the right channels could be online entertainment, email advertising, or visitor posting. An omnichannel approach might be best for boosting return on initial capital investment.

Crowd Division: One size doesn't fit all. Content ought to be custom-made to various crowd portions. By understanding the remarkable necessities and inclinations of different fragments, you can make content that resounds all the more really, prompting better return for money invested.

Visual Substance: Visual substance, like recordings, infographics, and pictures, frequently yields higher commitment rates contrasted with text-just satisfied. Integrating visual components into your substance procedure can prompt a huge lift in return for money invested.

Embolden (CTA): Clear and convincing CTAs guide your crowd to make the ideal move, for example, pursuing a pamphlet or making a buy. A successful CTA can altogether work on the return for capital invested of your substance promoting endeavors.

A/B Testing: Constantly testing and enhancing your substance, titles, CTAs, and different components can assist with recognizing what works best with your crowd. A/B testing can prompt more refined and return for capital invested driven content.

Content Advancement Spending plan: While natural reach is important, designating a spending plan for content advancement through paid promoting can expand your substance's span. This speculation can prompt higher return for capital invested, particularly when done in a calculated way.

Cutthroat Scene: Understanding what your rivals are doing as far as happy showcasing can give experiences into what works in your industry. It can assist you with adjusting your methodology for better return for capital invested.

Following and Examination: Strong following and investigation devices are fundamental for estimating the progress of your substance advertising endeavors. Breaking down key measurements like traffic, transformations, and client obtaining expenses can direct changes in accordance with further develop return for capital invested.

Content Newness: Obsolete substance can hurt your return on initial capital investment. Routinely refreshing and reusing old substances can assist with keeping up with its pertinence and adequacy over the long run.

Content Reusing: One piece of content can be reused into different arrangements. For instance, a blog entry can turn into a digital broadcast episode or a progression of online entertainment posts. This approach can boost the return for money invested of your unique substance.

Content Promoting Group: The abilities and aptitude of your substance showcasing group are pivotal. A talented group can think up and execute viable procedures that lead to higher return on initial capital investment.

Client Criticism: Paying attention to your crowd and integrating their criticism into your substance can make it more significant and locking in. This approach can prompt higher client maintenance and expanded return for capital invested.

Content Objectives: Setting clear, quantifiable objectives for your substance advertising endeavors is essential. Whether it's image mindfulness, lead age, or deals, adjusting your substance to explicit targets helps track return for money invested all the more really.

Content Lifecycle: Content doesn't have a static life expectancy. Various kinds of content, like evergreen and moving substances, have different life cycles. Understanding this can assist you with arranging your substance schedule and return on initial capital investment assumptions as needs be.

All in all, happy promoting return for capital invested is impacted by a large number of elements, every one of which requires cautious thought and vital preparation. By zeroing in on excellent, applicable substance, successful appropriation, crowd division, and persistent improvement, organizations can boost the profit from their substance showcasing speculations. It's essential to adjust and refine your technique after some time, as the advanced scene and shopper inclinations develop. At last, a happy showcasing return on initial capital investment isn't ensured, yet a thoroughly examined and executed technique extraordinarily works on the odds of coming out on top.

Content Quality and Relevance

In the present computerized age, content has turned into a foundation of correspondence, data dispersal, and showcasing. Whether you're a blogger, an entrepreneur, a virtual entertainment force to be reckoned with, or a substance maker, the quality and importance of your substance assume an essential part in deciding its prosperity. Content quality and importance are not simply trendy expressions; they are fundamental factors that can represent the deciding moment of your web-based presence and commitment. This article dives into the complexities of content quality and importance, making sense of their importance and offering tips on how to accomplish both.

The Significance of Content Quality:
Content quality is the establishment whereupon your computerized presence is constructed. It incorporates different components, like precision, uniqueness, comprehensibility, and worth to the crowd. Here are a few convincing motivations behind why content quality is of vital significance:

Credibility: Great substance lays out you as a tenable wellspring of data. At the point when your crowd realizes they can believe your substance, they are bound to draw in with it and offer it with others.

Website optimization Rankings: Web search tools like Google reward excellent substance with better rankings. On the off chance that your substance is well-informed, elegantly composed, and educational, it's bound to show up on the principal page of indexed lists, expanding your perceivability.

Crowd Commitment: Drawing in happy is bound to keep your crowd intrigued and urge them to invest more energy on your site or stage. This can bring about higher change rates and expanded client dependability.

Shareability: Quality substance is more shareable. Individuals are bound to share content that they view as significant, which can enhance your scope and impact.

Brand Picture: Your substance mirrors your image's picture. Top notch content can improve your image's standing, while low quality substance can discolor it.

The Meaning of Content Significance: Pertinence remains forever inseparable with quality. Content can be very much created, yet in the event that it's not applicable to your interest group, it may not yield the ideal outcomes. Here's the reason content pertinence is urgent:

Crowd Commitment: Applicable substance talks straightforwardly to the interests, needs, and worries of your crowd. It catches their consideration and keeps them locked in.

Personalization: In a time of personalization, conveying significant substance shows that you figure out your crowd and can take care of their singular inclinations.

Critical thinking: Important substance resolves the issues and questions your crowd has. This helps them as well as positions you as an issue solver and a significant asset.

Conversions: Pertinent substance can prompt higher transformation rates. At the point when your substance lines up with your crowd's necessities and interests, they are bound to make a move, whether it's making a buy, pursuing a pamphlet, or sharing your substance.

Techniques for Accomplishing Content Quality and Importance:

Now that we comprehend the significance of content quality and importance, how about we investigate methodologies to accomplish both:

Figure out Your Crowd: To make applicable substance, you really want to understand where your listeners might be coming from back to front. Direct crowd research, make purchaser personas, and draw in with your crowd through studies or virtual entertainment collaborations to acquire experiences into their inclinations and trouble spots.

Exhaustive Exploration: Quality substance requires intensive examination. Ensure your realities are precise, and your sources are tenable. Backing your substance with information and proof improves its quality and validity.

Clear cut Objectives: Characterize clear targets for your substance. What is it that you need to accomplish with each piece? Is it to illuminate, engage, or convince? Having explicit objectives as a main priority will direct your substance creation process.

Higher expectations without compromise: It's enticing to produce a high volume of content, however zeroing in on quality is better. Make content that offers genuine worth to your crowd, regardless of whether it implies distributing less every now and again.

Editing and Altering: Mistakes and linguistic blunders can right away diminish the nature of your substance. Continuously edit and alter your work prior to distributing. Consider utilizing instruments like Grammarly for help.

Consistency: Consistency in tone, style, and informing across your substance helps in building a brand personality. Your crowd ought to have the option to perceive your substance, even without seeing your logo.

Testing and Emphasis: Screen the presentation of your substance. Dissect what parts reverberate the most with your crowd, and utilize this criticism to refine your future substance technique.

Remain Refreshed: In the high speed advanced scene, patterns and interests can change rapidly. Remain refreshed with industry drifts and adjust your substance to stay applicable.

Content quality and importance are the mainstays of fruitful computerized correspondence. In a period where content is bountiful, standing apart requires a guarantee to creating top caliber, important substance that tends to your crowd's necessities and concerns. Whether you're a business planning to help deals or a blogger attempting to develop your readership, recollecting that quality and pertinence will separate you from the opposition and produce an enduring association with your crowd.

Target Audience and Persona

In the realm of promoting, publicizing, and content creation, the expressions "interest group" and "persona" are frequently utilized reciprocally. In any case, these two ideas fill particular needs and assume crucial parts in making effective methodologies for organizations and content makers the same. In this conversation, we will dive into the meaning of interest group and persona, investigating how they are characterized and the way in which they are utilized to associate with the target group.

Characterizing the Interest group

An interest group is a gathering of people who share normal qualities and characteristics that make them bound to be keen on an item, administration, or content. These common attributes might incorporate segment factors like age, orientation, area, and pay, as well as psychographic factors like interests, values, and way of life. Understanding your interest group is the underpinning of any viable showcasing technique, as it permits organizations and content makers to tailor their messages to reverberate with a particular gathering.

Distinguishing the main interest group is a multi-layered process that starts with statistical surveying. Organizations dissect information and lead reviews to acquire bits of knowledge into who their potential clients are. For example, an extravagance vehicle producer could distinguish its interest group as princely people matured 35-60, who have an inclination for premium cars and a higher discretionary cash flow.

The interest group is vital in figuring out where and how to successfully designate assets. It guides choices connected with item improvement, evaluating, appropriation, and showcasing channels. At the point when a business precisely recognizes its main interest group, it can abstain from squandering assets on contacting people who are probably not going to be keen on its contributions.

Grasping Personas

While the main interest group characterizes the more extensive gathering of possible clients, personas make this a stride further by making fictitious portrayals of individual individuals inside that crowd. Personas are definite person profiles that typify the qualities, inclinations, and ways of behaving of a particular section of the ideal interest group. They give a more profound comprehension of the crowd's necessities and inspirations.

Making personas includes digging into the mind of expected clients, going past socioeconomics to investigate psychographic factors. To go on with the case of the extravagance vehicle producer, a persona may "Find success Steve," a 45-year-old chief who values status and values top-level auto designing. This persona's profile would incorporate data about Steve's pay, interests, way of life, and even trouble spots connected with his ongoing vehicle.

Personas rejuvenate the interest group and assist organizations and content makers with making their messages more appealing and locking in. They act as an instrument to refine the crowd and guide content creation and promoting endeavors. At the point when a business comprehends the inclinations and issues of "Fruitful Steve," it can formulate content and showcasing systems that straightforwardly address his necessities, for example, featuring the vehicle's presentation and status bid.

The Collaboration Between Main interest group and Personas

The collaboration between the main interest group and personas is fundamental for making convincing, fully satisfied and advertising techniques. While the interest group characterizes the more extensive degree, personas give a more nuanced view. This is the way they cooperate:

Refining Content: Interest group bits of knowledge assist with deciding the overall subjects and messages, while personas give the granular subtleties. For example, an interest group of youthful experts could incorporate various personas like "Experience Searcher Alice" and "Eco-Cognizant Ethan." Every persona would illuminate content custom-made to their special advantages and values.

Personalization: Personas empower personalization on a more profound level. Content and advertising messages can be tweaked to reverberate with explicit personas inside the ideal interest group, causing the crowd to feel comprehended and esteemed.

Viable Advertising Channels: Realizing your ideal interest group's favored correspondence channels is essential, and personas assist with improving the substance for these channels. " Educated Tina" could answer well to computerized promotion, while "Conventional Tony" could favor regular postal mail.

Critical thinking: Personas are instrumental in tending to trouble spots. By understanding what inconveniences various personas, organizations can feature how their item or administration offers arrangements. For instance, if

"Family-Centered Fran" has worries about security, a vehicle producer can stress the vehicle's high level wellbeing highlights in promoting to that persona.

A valid example: Starbucks

To delineate the significance of the main interest group and personas, consider the instance of Starbucks, the worldwide café chain. Starbucks' interest group includes an extensive variety of old enough gatherings and socioeconomics, from understudies to experts to families. Notwithstanding, Starbucks has effectively used personas to associate with different portions of its ideal interest group.

For instance, one of Starbucks' personas may be "Morning Worker Mike." This persona addresses a moderately aged proficient who relies upon his everyday portion of caffeine to launch his day. Starbucks comprehends that Mike values comfort and speed, so they have created administrations like versatile requesting and drive-through eateries to take special care of his necessities. Their advertising messages and advancements are intended to interest his bustling way of life.

Then again, Starbucks likewise considers "Social Sarah," an undergrad who regularly visits their bistros to concentrate on meetings and get-togethers. For this persona, Starbucks offers comfortable and open to seating, free Wi-Fi, and occasional drinks that are well known among youthful grown-ups.

By making and taking care of different personas inside their assorted interest group, Starbucks has prevailed with regards to major areas of strength for building and client steadfastness across a wide range of clients.

Interest groups and personas are irreplaceable devices for viable correspondence in the realms of showcasing, promoting, and content creation. While the interest group characterizes the more extensive gathering of possible clients, personas reinvigorate that crowd by making nitty gritty person profiles. The cooperative energy between these ideas permits organizations and content makers to convey messages and items that are custom-made, engaging, and exceptionally powerful.

Distribution Channels, Timing and Consistency

The Mainstays of Fruitful Business Activities

In the always advancing scene of business, the significance of dispersion channels, timing, and consistency couldn't possibly be more significant. These three support points assume a vital part in the outcome of any undertaking, no matter what its size or industry. From the nearby bread shop to the worldwide tech monster, understanding how these components exchange can be the way to support development and productivity.

Circulation Channels: The Help of Business

Dispersion channels are the pathways through which items or administrations arrive at shoppers. They include a wide range of systems, from conventional retail locations and wholesalers to internet business stages and direct deals. Picking the right dispersion channels can represent the moment of truth choice for any business.

One of the principal contemplations while creating circulation channels is understanding the objective market. Where and how do potential clients like to shop? For example, an extravagance design brand could depend on restrictive stores in very good quality shopping locales to take special care of a select customer base, while a web-based book shop might use a site and organizations with worldwide delivery transporters to contact an expansive, geologically scattered crowd.

The planning of embracing and adjusting conveyance channels is basic. Innovation is an excellent driver around here. As internet business proceeds to develop and advance, organizations that neglect to embrace online dissemination channels might regard themselves as abandoned. Organizations like Amazon and Alibaba have upset customary retail conveyance, changing the manner in which buyers shop. Subsequently, organizations should stay lithe and versatile to stay applicable and serious.

Timing: The Quintessence of Significance

Timing is everything in business. Fruitful organizations comprehend their objective market as well as know when to enter it. The "perfect locations with impeccable timing" can launch a business to progress or prompt its death.

Development assumes a crucial part in timing. Consider Apple's presentation of the iPhone in 2007. It upset the cell phone industry and was delivered when buyers were eager for a gadget that could join music, web access, and correspondence. The planning of this item allowed Apple to catch a huge piece of the pie and set up a good foundation for itself as a tech monster.

In the domain of innovation, the "early adopter" idea is likewise important. A few organizations flourish by focusing on shoppers who enthusiastically embrace new items or administrations. Early reception can be a high-risk, high-reward methodology, as it requires weighty speculation and development. Be that as it may, it can prompt market authority and supportable development when executed actually.

In addition, timing isn't restricted to item dispatches. Showcasing efforts, deals advancements, and even venture into new business sectors require conscious thought of timing. A very much coordinated promoting effort can make a buzz around an item, driving interest and producing deals.

Consistency: The Bedrock of Trust

The fact that binds business tasks makes consistency the magic. It assembles entrust with clients, representatives, and partners. It guarantees that shoppers have a solid encounter when they draw in with a brand. A reliable brand is a dependable brand.

For shoppers, consistency implies getting a similar degree of value and administration each time they collaborate with a business. Take the case of Starbucks. Whether you request a latte in New York or Tokyo, you can anticipate a similar taste and quality. This consistency breeds client devotion and makes a solid standing.

Consistency isn't restricted to items or administrations; it reaches out to an organization's qualities, informing, and marking. At the point when a business imparts its qualities reliably and adjusts its activities to these qualities, it constructs entrust with clients. Irregularities in informing or activities can prompt disarray and disintegrate trust.

Inward consistency is similarly significant. Representatives ought to comprehend and embrace an organization's qualities and mission. At the point when an organization's inner culture is steady with its outer picture, it cultivates reliability among workers and drives hierarchical achievement. A steady corporate culture is a major component of a solid and useful labor force.

All in all, dissemination channels, timing, and consistency are fundamental to the progress of any business. Dispersion channels decide how an item arrives at the customer, timing directs when and how it does as such, and consistency constructs trust and unwavering quality. These three points of support ought to be painstakingly thought of, incorporated, and executed to make major areas of strength for a strong business establishment. Organizations that face these components are better prepared to explore the steadily changing scene of business and lay down a good foundation for themselves as pioneers in their separate ventures.

Chapter 4
Case Studies and Successful Content Marketing ROI Examples

Contextual investigations and Fruitful Substance Promoting return for capital invested Models

Content showcasing has arisen as an indispensable system for organizations to interface with their crowds, fabricate memorability, and at last drive income. The outcome of content promotion is in many cases estimated by its profit from speculation (return on initial capital investment). In this article, we'll investigate the meaning of contextual analyses in satisfied showcasing and feature a few eminent instances of organizations that have accomplished great return for capital invested through their substance promoting endeavors.

The Force of Contextual analyses

Contextual analyses are a vital device in happy advertising because of multiple factors. They act as convincing stories that give proof of the viability of a specific system or approach. At the point when organizations can feature true instances of how their substance advertising endeavors yielded positive outcomes, it imparts trust in expected clients and clients.

1. HubSpot's Inbound Promoting Achievement

HubSpot, a forerunner in inbound promotion, has been a trailblazer in satisfying showcasing. They've reliably exhibited the worth of their inbound promoting technique through contextual investigations. HubSpot made an inside and out contextual investigation on how they assisted one client with expanding site traffic by 2,500%, creating 8,500 leads, and lifting income by 6,000%.

This contextual analysis delineates the viability of HubSpot's administrations as well as gives significant bits of knowledge into how inbound promotion can deliver substantial outcomes for organizations.

2. Red Bull's Substance System

Red Bull, the caffeinated drink monster, has constructed a substance promoting realm around outrageous games and experience. Their most well known content promoting drive is Red Bull Stratos, where Felix Baumgartner broke the sound wall with a drop from the edge of room. Red Bull's contextual analysis on this occasion subtleties how it created enormous web-based commitment, expanded brand mindfulness, and prompted a flood in deals.

Red Bull's prosperity demonstrates the way that remarkable and extraordinary substance can dazzle crowds, produce viral buzz, and convert into significant return for capital invested.

Effective Substance Advertising return on initial capital investment Models

Presently, how about we plunge into a few certifiable instances of organizations that have accomplished striking return for money invested through satisfied promoting:

1. GoPro - Client Produced Content

GoPro, the activity camera maker, has utilized client created content for its potential benefit. By empowering clients to share their completely exhilarating experiences and tricks caught with GoPro cameras, the organization made a broad library of invigorating, client created content.

This content fills in as true tributes as well as rouses and connects with their interest group. GoPro revealed a 73% year-over-year development in Q4 income, displaying how content showcasing can straightforwardly add to the main concern.

2. Coca-Cola - Content That Pulls at the Heartstrings

Coca-Cola's substance promoting endeavors are eminent for their close to home reverberation. Quite possibly their best mission, "Offer a Coke," involved printing individuals' names on Coke bottles, empowering clients to impart a Coke to loved ones.

This mission created inescapable virtual entertainment sharing, with clients posting pictures of Coke bottles with their names on them. It prompted a huge lift in brand commitment and, at last, deals.

3. Dollar Shave Club - Viral Video

Dollar Shave Club stirred things up in the razor business with a low-financial plan viral video. In the video, the pioneer made sense of the advantages of Dollar Shave Club's reasonable, excellent razors in a funny and engaging way.

The video immediately became a web sensation, collecting a great many perspectives and prompting a flood in memberships. Dollar Shave Club was consequently obtained by Unilever for a billion bucks, exhibiting the uncommon return on initial capital investment that inventive substances can convey.

4. Support - Instructive Contributing to a blog

Support, a web-based entertainment the executives instrument, took on a substance promoting methodology revolved around instructive writing for a blog. They distributed an abundance of content that offered important experiences and tips via web-based entertainment and content showcasing.

Cushion's blog laid out them as thought pioneers as well as drawn in a committed following. The organization saw a huge expansion in both rush hour gridlock and memberships, converting into significant income development.

These contextual analyses and fruitful substance advertising return for money invested models show the extraordinary influence of first rate satisfied promoting procedures. In our current reality where shoppers are immersed with promoting, content showcasing offers a more legitimate and connecting way for brands to interface with their crowd.

By utilizing contextual analyses, organizations can give substantial proof of the return for money invested capability of their substance promoting endeavors.

Whether it's through client produced content, profound narrating, viral recordings, or instructive contributing to a blog, these models demonstrate the way that inventive and designated content can prompt huge income development.

Content advertising isn't just about making content; it's tied in with making content that associates, reverberates, and, above all, changes over.

In the present cutthroat scene, the capacity to grandstand these examples of overcoming adversity through contextual investigations and models is a critical driver for organizations hoping to capitalize on their substance promoting speculations.

Lessons Learned from Failed Attempts on Content Marketing

Content showcasing is an essential instrument for organizations looking to lay out areas of strength for a presence, connect with their crowd, and drive income. Nonetheless, it's an excursion loaded up with preliminaries and mistakes, and numerous examples are gained from bombed endeavors. In this 700-word investigation, we'll dive into the absolute most basic examples that can be gathered from fruitless introductions to content promoting.

Misjudging the Force of Technique:

Quite possibly the most well-known trap in satisfied promotion is jumping heedlessly without an unmistakable procedure. Numerous organizations make content heedlessly, trusting something will stick. Bombed endeavors frequently come from this absence of arranging. A distinct methodology, including crowd examination, content schedule, and key execution pointers (KPIs), is the foundation of fruitful substance showcasing.

Dismissing Crowd Exploration:

A basic part of content showcasing is grasping your ideal interest group. Disappointment frequently happens when organizations don't focus on crowd research. What is it that they need? What issues might your substance at any point settle for them? Without replies to these inquiries, your substance might come up short.

Better standards without ever compromising:

A typical confusion is that the more satisfied, the better. This conviction can prompt substance exhaustion, where crowds become overpowered and withdrawn. Zeroing in on better standards when in doubt is urgent. Well-informed, elegantly composed, and important substance reverberates more with your crowd.

Disregarding Website optimization:

Website streamlining (Web optimization) is a fundamental part of content promotion. Dismissing it can bring about your substance becoming mixed up in the immense advanced scene. Legitimate Website design enhancement works on, including watchword research and on-page improvement, are fundamental for content perceivability.

Conflicting Distributing:

Conflicting distribution can confound your crowd and block your substance showcasing endeavors. It's vital to keep a normal distributing timetable to keep your crowd connected with and lay out trust.

Neglecting to Adjust:

The advanced scene is continually developing, and content showcasing procedures should adjust to these changes. Many bombed endeavors happen in light of the fact that organizations neglect to change in accordance with recent fads and advances. Remaining current and it is significant to be available for advancement.

Not Estimating Results:

Content showcasing without estimating results is like cruising without a compass. To improve, you want to understand what's working and so forth. Dissect information and KPIs to comprehend which content is resounding with your crowd and which needs improvement.

Absence of Tolerance:

Content promoting is a drawn out methodology. A few organizations leave their endeavors rashly on the off chance that they don't see prompt outcomes. It's fundamental to be patient and comprehend that achievement frequently requires some investment to appear.

Inability to Advance Substance:

Making content is just a single piece of the situation. It is similarly vital to Advance it. Inability to advance substance through online entertainment, email promoting, and different directives can bring about restricted reach and effect.

Inauthenticity:

Crowds rush to distinguish inauthentic substances. In the event that your substance doesn't line up with your image's qualities or on the other hand on the off chance that it seems tricky, it can prompt a deficiency of trust and commitment.

Disregarding Client Criticism:

Clients frequently give important criticism that can illuminate your substance procedure. Overlooking their remarks, questions, and concerns can prompt a distinction between your substance and your crowd.

Inability to Enhance Content Sorts:

Assortment is the zest of content promoting. Zeroing in exclusively on one sort of happiness, for example, blog entries, can prompt stagnation. Differentiate your substance by including recordings, infographics, digital broadcasts, and different arrangements to keep your crowd locked in.

Sitting above Contender Examination:

Contender examination is a gold mine of bits of knowledge. Inability to screen your rivals' substance systems can bring about botched open doors and insufficient methodologies.

Overlooking Portable Enhancement:

With most of web traffic coming from cell phones, neglecting to upgrade your substance for portable can be negative. Versatile responsive plan is basic for coming to and drawing in with your crowd.

No Unmistakable Source of inspiration:

A substance piece without an unmistakable source of inspiration (CTA) resembles a boat without an objective. Each piece of content ought to direct the peruser toward a particular activity, whether it's buying in, sharing, or making a buy.

All in all, bombed endeavors in happy promoting can be significant opportunities for growth. They shed light on the basic parts of technique, crowd understanding, and transformation to a consistently developing advanced scene. By noticing these illustrations and staying away from these normal traps, organizations can diagram a more effective course in their substance promoting endeavors. Content showcasing is a unique field, and the people who gain from their errors are best situated to flourish in it.

Chapter 5
Strategies for Improving Content Marketing ROI

Systems for Further developing Substance Advertising return for capital invested

Presentation

Content promoting is a fundamental part of a fruitful computerized showcasing system. It includes making and disseminating significant substance to draw in and connect with your interest group. Nonetheless, to boost its effect, you really want to zero in on further developing your Substance Advertising Profit from Venture (return for capital invested). In this article, we will investigate different systems that can assist you with upgrading your substance promoting return for capital invested.

Crowd Exploration and Persona Advancement

Prior to making content, understanding your interest group is vital. Lead inside and out examination to distinguish their inclinations, problem areas, and necessities. Foster purchaser personas to make content that reverberates with your optimal clients. The better you understand what your listeners might be thinking, the more powerful your substance will be.

Great Substance Creation

Make content that is educational, pertinent, and locking in. Great substance draws in your crowd as well as makes them want more and more. Put resources into proficient journalists, planners, and videographers to create content that hangs out in a jam-packed web-based space.

Reliable Marking

Keep a reliable brand picture and voice across the entirety of your substance. A strong brand character fabricates trust and makes your substance more conspicuous. This aids in holding existing clients and drawing in new ones.

Content Advancement for Web optimization

Website improvement (Web optimization) assumes a fundamental part in satisfied showcasing. Enhance your substance for web search tools to guarantee that it contacts a more extensive crowd. Utilize significant catchphrases, meta labels, and excellent backlinks to work on your substance's perceivability in query items.

Dispersion Procedure

Making uncommon substances is only a piece of the battle.You should likewise have a very much arranged dissemination methodology. Utilize different stages, for example, virtual entertainment, email advertising, and content partnership to arrive at your main interest group where they are generally dynamic.

Email Promoting

Email promoting is an integral asset for content dissemination and crowd commitment. Fabricate an email list and send customary bulletins with important substance. This can assist with supporting leads, direct people to your site, and further develop return for capital invested.

Content Advancement

Advance your substance through paid publicizing on stages like Google Advertisements and virtual entertainment. This can assist you with contacting a more extensive crowd and drive designated traffic to your site.

Content Schedule

Make a substance schedule to plan and timetable your substance ahead of time. This guarantees that you have a predictable progression of content over time. An efficient schedule likewise assists you with adjusting your substance to occasional patterns and promoting efforts.

Investigation and Estimation Use examination instruments to follow the introduction of your substance.Distinguish what works and what doesn't. This information driven approach permits you to settle on informed choices and improve your substance promoting procedure for better return for capital invested.

A/B Testing

Try different things with various substance configurations, titles, and invitations to take action (CTAs) utilizing A/B testing. This assists you with recognizing which components reverberate most with your crowd and refine your substance as needs be.

Client produced Content

Urge your clients to make and share their substance connected with your items or administrations. Client produced content forms trust as well as lessens your substance creation costs.

Content Reusing

Try not to allow your incredible content to go to squander. Reuse it into different arrangements, for example, blog entries, infographics, recordings, and digital broadcasts. This augments the worth of your substance and arrives at various fragments of your crowd.

Force to be reckoned with Advertising

Influence forces to be reckoned with in your specialty to advance your substance. They can assist you with contacting a more extensive and more drawn in crowd. Team up with powerhouses who line up with your image and values.

Remarketing

Use remarketing methods to target clients who have recently communicated with your substance or site. This keeps your image top of mind and supports transformations.

Change Rate Improvement (CRO)

Guarantee that your site is improved for changes. A very much planned and easy to use site can fundamentally influence your substance promoting return for money invested by transforming guests into clients.

Client Input

Pay attention to your clients' input and change your substance system as needs be. Address their interests, answer their inquiries, and make content that takes care of their necessities.

Social Tuning in

Screen web-based entertainment stages for discussions connected with your image and industry. Partake in conversations, answer questions, and offer your substance where significant. This forms your position and trust.

Content Adaptation

Investigate chances to adapt your substance straightforwardly or in a roundabout way. For instance, you can offer premium substance behind a paywall, sell stock connected with your substance, or utilize content to advance partner items and procure commissions.

Further developing Substance Promoting return on initial capital investment is a continuous interaction that requires commitment and versatility. By following these systems, you can make a more successful substance promoting procedure that conveys improved results and better yields on your speculation. Remember that outcome in happy showcasing takes time, persistence, and persistent improvement.

Content Optimization and Audience

In the tremendous computerized scene of the 21st 100 years, content rules. It is the backbone of sites, web-based entertainment, and each stage that tries to draw in a group of people. However, making content alone isn't sufficient; it should be improved to reverberate with the target group. This article investigates the unpredictable dance of content advancement and crowd commitment, revealing insight into the procedures and strategies that overcome any issues among makers and their watchers.

Figuring out Happy Improvement

Content streamlining is the specialty of refining advanced content to upgrade its perceivability, significance, and generally execution. A multi-layered process considers different variables, including website improvement (Web optimization), client experience, and content quality.

SEO: At the core of content advancement is Web optimization, which is the most common way of fitting substance to be web index agreeable. Watchwords, meta labels, and very much organized content are principal to further developing a site's positioning on web index results pages. Content makers should distinguish applicable watchwords and integrate them normally into their substance. This essential situation guarantees that web search tools list and rank the substance for these watchwords.

Client Experience: Client experience (UX) is critical in happy improvement. A very much organized, easy to use site with quick stacking times and clear route improves the client's insight. These components please the crowd as well as thought about emphatically via web search tools. Connecting with visuals and responsive planning can likewise keep the crowd on the page longer, indicating to web indexes that the substance is important.

Content Quality: Quality is non-debatable. Content should be useful, precise, and elegantly composed. Connecting with content keeps the crowd perusing as well as energizes sharing, which can extend the substance's span. Furthermore, top notch content lays out power and validity in a given specialty, making it more probable that others will connect to it.

Associating with the Right Crowd

Whenever content is streamlined, guiding it towards the right audience is fundamental. Distinguishing and understanding the interest group is pivotal for creating content that resounds. Here are a few methodologies for interfacing with the right crowd:

Crowd Exploration: Start by directing exhaustive crowd research. Comprehend their socioeconomics, interests, problem areas, and requirements. Apparatuses like Google Examination and web-based entertainment bits of knowledge give important information on crowd conduct.

Purchaser Personas: Foster purchaser personas to make an unmistakable image of your optimal crowd. This includes making definite profiles that incorporate age, orientation, interests, and, surprisingly, theoretical situations. These personas assist with satisfying makers tailor their work to suit the requirements and inclinations of the crowd.

Segmentation: Not all crowd individuals are something very similar. Use crowd division to classify watchers in light of different variables, like their stage in the purchaser's excursion or their cooperation history with your substance. This takes into account exceptionally designated content that talks straightforwardly to the crowd's requirements.

Commitment Investigation: Screen and examine crowd commitment with your substance. Which points create the most interest? What kind of satisfaction is shared the most? By understanding these examples, content makers can create a greater amount of what resounds with the crowd.

The Marriage of Content Advancement and Crowd Commitment

Content advancement and crowd commitment are not independent procedures; they supplement and support one another. This is the way they blend:

Content Custom-made to the Crowd: Content advancement guarantees that the substance contacts the crowd by further developing its web search tool perceivability. At the point when the crowd looks for explicit watchwords, upgraded content is bound to show up in the query items.

Personalization: Content can be customized in view of crowd information. For example, a web based business site can show item proposals custom-made to individual clients. Personalization upgrades client experience and energizes commitment.

Criticism Circles: Empower crowd cooperation through remarks, audits, and virtual entertainment discussions. This criticism circle gives important experiences that can be utilized to additionally enhance content. It likewise makes a feeling of the local area and having a place, fortifying the association between satisfied maker and crowd.

Iterative Improvement: Content improvement is a continuous interaction. Routinely screen the exhibition of content, track crowd commitment, and adjust as needs be. It's a pattern of nonstop improvement where crowd criticism illuminates enhancement endeavors, and streamlined content better draws in the crowd.

All in all, satisfied streamlining and crowd commitment are cut out of the same cloth in the computerized world. Viable substance streamlining guarantees that content contacts its target group, while crowd commitment makes them want more and more. By making content that talks straightforwardly to the necessities and interests of the crowd, makers can fabricate a steadfast and drawn following. In this steadily developing scene, this collaboration is the way to progress.

Engagement Strategies, A/B Testing and Iteration

In the quick moving and steadily advancing scene of computerized showcasing, remaining on the ball is fundamental for progress. Among the many instruments and strategies available to an advertiser, three stand apart as pivotal parts of any viable computerized promoting effort: Commitment Techniques, A/B Testing, and Cycle. In this 800-word investigation, we will dive into every one of these methodologies, featuring their importance and the cooperative relationship that ties them together.

Commitment Systems: The Establishment

Commitment systems are the bedrock whereupon fruitful advanced showcasing efforts are fabricated. These systems include a scope of procedures intended to catch the consideration of a crowd of people, invigorate their advantage, and urge them to connect with a brand or item. Such connection can take many structures, from preferences, remarks, and offers via web-based entertainment to snaps and transformations on a site.

One of the foundations of commitment techniques is content creation. Significant, applicable, and enlightening substance is vital to drawing in and holding the consideration of likely clients. Narrating, specifically, has acquired conspicuousness as a strong commitment system. Stories enrapture and resound with individuals on a profound level, empowering a brand to produce a close to home association with its crowd.

Past happy, commitment systems likewise incorporate local area building. Brands are progressively zeroing in on making and sustaining networks around their items or administrations. Online gatherings, web-based entertainment gatherings, and intuitive live meetings have all become well known apparatuses for encouraging these networks. Drawing in with clients in this way helps construct trust and brand devotion.

Integrating video content is another convincing commitment technique. Recordings, whether short clasps or inside and out narratives, give a vivid encounter, making it simpler to pass on data and bring out feelings. With the ascent of stages like YouTube and TikTok, video showcasing has turned into a focal part of commitment techniques.

While there is no one size-fits-all way to deal with commitment systems, personalization is turning out to be progressively significant. Customized content and offers take special care of the singular requirements and inclinations of clients, guaranteeing that they feel seen and heard. This can prompt higher commitment and better transformation rates.

A/B Testing: The Way to Enhancement

When a commitment system is set up, the following basic step is A/B testing. A/B testing includes contrasting two renditions of a site page, email, promotion, or some other component of a showcasing effort to figure out which one performs better. This procedure is essential for improving advanced promoting endeavors.

The idea is clear: you make two marginally various renditions of a component, with one being the control (A) and the other the variation (B). The two variants are then introduced to approach sections of the interest group, and their corporations are estimated and examined. By contrasting the exhibition of An and B, advertisers can settle on information driven conclusions about what works best.

A/B testing can be applied to different parts of a computerized showcasing effort. It can assist with refining the design and plan of a presentation page, decide the best phrasing for a source of inspiration (CTA), or evaluate the effect of various variety plans in an email crusade. Indeed, even the littlest changes can essentially affect client conduct, and A/B testing uncovers which changes merit carrying out.

The strength of A/B testing lies in its objectivity. It eliminates mystery and instinct from the dynamic cycle. Advertisers can depend on information to pursue informed decisions about what reverberates most with their crowd. As well as further developing commitment, A/B testing can prompt expanded transformations, decreased skip rates, and higher income.

Additionally, A/B testing is definitely not a one-time movement. An iterative cycle ought to be progressing. As crowd inclinations and ways of behaving develop, so too should advertising techniques. Persistently testing and enhancing content and plan components keeps a mission new and cutthroat.

Iteration: The Development of Achievement

Cycle is the regular continuation of A/B testing and is, truth be told, the foundation of any successful computerized promoting effort. In a quickly changing computerized scene, advertisers should be ready to adjust and develop their techniques over the long run. This versatility is where emphasis becomes an integral factor.

Iterative promotion includes the efficient survey and refinement of showcasing endeavors in view of information and experiences acquired from A/B testing and other examinations. It's tied in with gaining from triumphs and disappointments, and utilizing that information to make a more compelling effort. The objective isn't simply to streamline for the ongoing second however to be ready for future patterns and difficulties.

A critical part of emphasis is remaining receptive to the most recent computerized promoting patterns and innovations. As new stages and devices arise, they can furnish energizing chances to draw in with clients in new and imaginative ways. By consistently testing and adjusting, a brand can remain significant and jump all over new chances as they emerge.

Cycle additionally stretches out to crowd division. As a brand's client base develops, so should the manner in which it fragments its crowd. Figuring out the changing socioeconomics and psychographics of the objective market is vital for fitting substance and offers to explicit client fragments. This personalization improves commitment and energizes reliability.

All in all, Commitment Systems, A/B Testing, and Cycle structure a ternion that powers fruitful computerized promoting efforts. Commitment systems establish the groundwork by catching and holding the consideration of a group of people. A/B testing gives the resources to improve crusade components and refine them in light of information driven experiences. At long last, emphasis guarantees that a promoting effort stays versatile and receptive to changing patterns and crowd inclinations.

This harmonious relationship among these three components is the way to exploring the unique universe of computerized promoting effectively. Brands that put resources into commitment methodologies, A/B testing, and progressing cycle are better outfitted to interface with their crowd, drive changes, and remain ahead in a steadily developing scene.

Chapter 6
Challenges and Obstacles,Com mon Pitfalls in ROI Analysis Dealing with Uncertainty

Profit from Venture (return for capital invested) examination is a basic device for dynamic in both business and individual accounting. It gives an organized structure to assessing the monetary advantages and expenses of a venture. Notwithstanding, the way to leading a solid return on initial capital investment investigation is frequently full of difficulties and impediments, particularly while managing vulnerability. In this paper, we will investigate the normal traps that emerge while surveying return for money invested in questionable conditions and examine methodologies to relieve these difficulties.

Difficulties and Snags:
Wrong Information:
One of the key difficulties in return for capital invested examination is the

exactness of information. Assuming that the underlying information inputs are inaccurate or deficient, the whole investigation can be defective. Vulnerability further fuels this issue, as it frequently prompts suppositions that can prompt mistakes in projections. To moderate this test, it is crucial to accumulate however much exact and applicable information as could be expected, while recognizing the innate vulnerability and possible predispositions in the information.

Questionable Economic situations:

Monetary circumstances and market elements are continually evolving. Return on initial capital investment examination normally depends on suppositions about future incomes, which can be exceptionally dubious in a unique market. Business speculations and monetary choices need to represent the inborn capriciousness of economic situations. This is much of the time done through responsiveness investigation, where the return on initial capital investment is determined under different situations to grasp the scope of likely results.

Time Skylines:

Deciding the fitting time skyline for a return for money invested investigation is a critical test. The more extended the time skyline, the more questionable the projections become. Then again, a brief time frame skyline may not catch the genuine worth of a venture. Finding some kind of harmony between present moment and long haul viewpoints is essential, and chiefs ought to be careful about over-depending on long haul projections despite vulnerability.

Normal Entanglements:
Dismissing Hazard Evaluation:
One normal trap is neglecting to integrate risk evaluation into the return for capital invested investigation. Vulnerability suggests risk, and the inability to represent this hazard can prompt excessively hopeful projections. Methods, for example, Monte Carlo reenactments, which model different potential results in view of probabilistic dispersions, can assist with resolving this issue. It gives a more practical perspective on the scope of potential return for capital invested results.

Overconfidence:
Pomposity is a mental inclination that can prompt excessively hopeful return on initial capital investment gauges. Individuals will generally be more positive about their decisions than the precision of those decisions warrants. Notwithstanding vulnerability, it's critical to recognize the impediments of our insight and presumptions, and to apply a more safe methodology while assessing returns.

Disregarding the Expense of Capital:
The expense of capital is the return expected by financial backers or the loan cost on acquired reserves. A typical entanglement is neglecting the expense of capital while assessing return for money invested. This prompts the supposition that any sure return on initial capital investment is satisfactory. Truly, a speculation should give a return more prominent than the expense of money to be monetarily legitimized. Neglecting to consider this can bring about misdirecting return for money invested estimations.

Disregarding Opportunity Expenses:
Opportunity costs are the inescapable gets back from picking one venture over another. While leading return on initial capital investment examination, people and organizations frequently ignore these expenses. Vulnerability can worsen this issue by making it hard to survey whether an elective speculation would have been a superior decision. A careful investigation ought to consider the open door costs related to various speculation choices.

Preference for non threatening information:
Tendency to look for predictable answers is the inclination to search out and incline toward data that affirms one's assumptions. In return for capital invested examination, this predisposition can prompt specifically utilizing information that upholds an ideal result while disregarding problematic data. In questionable conditions, tendency to look for predictable answers can bring about imperfect direction. It is fundamental to stay open to a scope of likely results and to assess all suitable data basically.

Managing Vulnerability:
Situation Examination:
One powerful way to deal with managing vulnerability in return on initial capital investment examination is situation examination. This includes making various situations with various suspicions and evaluating the return for capital invested under every situation. Thus, chiefs gain a more clear comprehension of the scope of potential results, which can illuminate better independent direction.

Responsiveness Investigation:

Responsiveness examination includes transforming each factor in turn while keeping others steady to perceive how delicate the return on initial capital investment is to various data sources. This distinguishes which factors altogether affect return for capital invested. By zeroing in on these key factors, chiefs can make more educated decisions in the face regarding vulnerability.

Genuine Choices Investigation:

Genuine choices examination broadens return for money invested investigation by considering the worth of adaptability in direction. In questionable conditions, having the choice to delay, extend, or leave a speculation can be profoundly important. By integrating genuine choices into the investigation, leaders can more readily represent vulnerability and adjust their techniques as needs be.

Well-qualified Sentiments and Outer Approval:

Talking with specialists in the significant field or looking for outside approval from fair sources can give important bits of knowledge into the exactness of presumptions and projections. This outside information can assist with lessening inclinations and work on the dependability of return for capital invested investigation.

Return for capital invested examination is a significant instrument for settling on informed monetary choices, yet it accompanies its reasonable portion of difficulties and traps, particularly while managing vulnerability. Wrong information, questionable economic situations, and mental predispositions can all sabotage the unwavering quality of return for money invested estimations. In any case, by consolidating risk appraisal, utilizing different examination strategies, and staying open to outer approval, leaders can all the more likely explore the vulnerability that encompasses return on initial capital investment examination and go with additional educated decisions.

Chapter 7
Future Trends in Content Marketing ROI

Content showcasing has turned into a fundamental piece of advanced prompting systems, and its development is continually molded by arising patterns and innovations. One of the basic measurements that organizations use to quantify the viability of their substance showcasing endeavors is Profit from Speculation (return for capital invested). Understanding what's in store patterns in happily promoting return on initial capital investment is fundamental for remaining cutthroat and augmenting the effect of your substance crusades.

1. Information Driven Independent direction:
The eventual fate of content advertising return on initial capital investment will be

intensely affected by information driven navigation. With the rising accessibility of information investigation devices, organizations can acquire further experiences into how their substance is performing. This incorporates following client commitment, change rates, and even feeling investigation. By saddling the force of information, content advertisers can arrive at informed conclusions about what content to deliver and how to upgrade their methodologies for better return for money invested.

2. Personalization:

Personalization is certainly not another idea in happy promotion, yet its significance is developing. Fitting substance to individual inclinations and ways of behaving can altogether further develop return for money invested.

As simulated intelligence and AI innovations keep on propelling, content personalization will turn out to be more complex. Advertisers will actually want to make content that resounds with explicit crowd fragments, prompting higher commitment and change rates.

3. Video Predominance:

Video content has been on the ascent for a long time, and this pattern is supposed to proceed. Later on, video will assume a much more critical part in satisfying showcasing.

Recordings are connecting with, shareable, and viable at passing on complex data in a short measure of time. Content advertisers who can saddle the force of video will probably see higher return for money invested.

4. Intuitive Substance:

Intuitive substance, for example, tests, surveys, and reviews, is turning out to be progressively famous. It energizes client cooperation and commitment, which can prompt better return on initial capital investment. Intuitive substance is likewise important for social affair information on client inclinations and conduct, assisting advertisers with refining their techniques.

5. Voice Inquiry Advancement:

The ascent of voice-enacted gadgets and voice scan has suggestions for content promoting. Improving substance for voice search will be vital for keeping an upper hand. Voice look will quite often be more conversational, and content advertisers should adjust their systems to successfully give replies to these questions.

6. Increased Reality (AR) and Augmented Reality (VR):

AR and VR advancements are having an impact on how content is made and consumed. These innovations give vivid encounters that can be utilized for the end goal of promoting.

For instance, organizations can utilize AR to permit clients to take a stab at virtual items or investigate a computerized display area. While the reception of AR and VR might in any case be in its beginning phases, it holds guarantee for improving substance promoting return for capital invested.

7. Content Robotization:

The mechanization of content creation is as of now a reality somewhat with the utilization of chatbots and simulated intelligence produced content. Later on, we can expect more complex substance mechanization instruments that can make top caliber, applicable substances at scale.

While this might raise worries about the genuineness of content, when utilized mindfully, it can upgrade return for money invested by lessening creation costs and expanding content result.

8. Social Business:

Web-based entertainment stages are progressively coordinating shopping highlights, permitting clients to buy items straightforwardly from social posts. Content advertisers should adjust their procedures to capitalize on friendly business valuable open doors. This shift can possibly further develop return for capital invested by decreasing erosion in the client venture.

9. Maintainability and Reason Driven Content:

Customers are progressively aware of ecological and social issues. Content showcasing that lines up with an organization's supportability and social obligation drives can resound with crowds. Content that advances a reason driven message can prompt higher commitment and reliability, eventually influencing return for money invested.

10. Content Estimation and Attribution:

Crediting the effect of explicit substance pieces on return on initial capital investment has been difficult for advertisers. Later on, we can expect further developed attribution models that consider the whole client venture. This will empower content advertisers to all the more likely comprehend which content contributes most to transformations and return for money invested.

11. Security Guidelines and Information Assurance:

As security guidelines like GDPR and CCPA keep on advancing, content advertisers should adjust their systems to agree with these principles. This might influence how information is gathered and utilized, yet it's fundamental for keeping up with entrust with customers and staying away from likely legitimate issues.

12. Content Quality and Authority:

Later on, web crawlers and clients will put a much more noteworthy accentuation on the quality and authority of content. Delivering well-informed, definitive substance that offers genuine worth to the crowd will be fundamental for keeping up with high inquiry rankings and driving natural traffic, at last influencing return on initial capital investment.

All in all, patterns in satisfied advertising return on initial capital investment are formed by innovation, information, and moving shopper ways of behaving. Content advertisers should adjust to these progressions to amplify the effect of their methodologies.

Information driven navigation, personalization, and the ascent of video and intelligent substance will keep on being at the very front of fruitful substance promoting.

Moreover, rising advances like AR, VR, and voice search, as well as the coordination of manageability and social obligation, will all assume critical parts in molding content showcasing return for capital invested in the years to come.

Emerging Technologies and Data Privacy and Ethics

In the computerized age, we are seeing a phenomenal multiplication of arising advancements that are reshaping the manner in which we live, work, and impart. While these developments hold the commitment of extraordinary headways in different areas, they additionally raise huge worries with respect to information protection and morals. The interconnected universe of arising innovations and information protection is a complex and consistently developing scene that requests cautious thought and moral watchfulness.

Arising Innovations: An Extraordinary Power

Arising advancements incorporate many developments, including man-made consciousness (computer based intelligence), AI, blockchain, 5G, the Web of Things (IoT), and quantum figuring, among others. These advancements can possibly alter ventures and engage social orders in various ways. For example, simulated intelligence and AI can upgrade clinical conclusions, work on monetary examination, and robotize fabricating processes.

Blockchain innovation offers straightforward and secure answers for supply chains and monetary exchanges, while 5G and IoT vow to make more brilliant, more associated urban communities and frameworks. Quantum figuring can possibly take care of perplexing issues at speeds unbelievable by the present norms.

The fast reception of these innovations is being driven by their capability to further develop effectiveness, set out new monetary open doors, and address a portion of the world's most squeezing difficulties. Notwithstanding, as these developments keep on multiplying, worries about information protection and morals have become progressively integral to the discussion.

Information Security: A Central Right

Information security is the right of people to control and safeguard their own data. During a time of large information, it has become more basic than any other time to shield the delicate information gathered by legislatures, associations, and computerized stages. Arising advances, while offering critical advantages, present new dangers to information security.

One of the essential information protection concerns is the assortment and abuse of individual data. In the time of man-made intelligence and AI, tremendous measures of information are accumulated, dissected, and used to foster complex profiles of people.

This information can be utilized for customized promoting, however it can likewise be taken advantage of for additional accursed purposes, for example, controlling popular assessment or participating in cyberattacks. Finding some kind of harmony between information assortment and security assurance is a continuous test.

Besides, the Web of Things makes plenty of interconnected gadgets that continually gather information from our regular routines. While this interconnectedness offers comfort, it likewise raises worries about who approaches this information and the way things are gotten.

For instance, savvy home gadgets that screen your exercises can be powerless against hacking, possibly uncovering touchy data or in any event, undermining your actual security.

Morals in Arising Advancements

The turn of events and utilization of arising innovations likewise lead to a large group of moral predicaments. One of the essential worries is the potential for predisposition and segregation in simulated intelligence frameworks.

Simulated intelligence calculations are much of the time prepared on information that may as of now contain predispositions, and while perhaps not painstakingly observed, these inclinations can sustain separation in different regions, from recruiting cycles to law enforcement choices.

Guaranteeing that simulated intelligence frameworks are planned and prepared to be fair and straightforward is a huge test that technologists and policymakers should address.

One more moral concern includes the rising computerization of occupations. While arising advances can improve effectiveness and efficiency, they can likewise uproot human laborers. The moral inquiry is the way society ought to deal with the removal of laborers and what measures ought to be set up to guarantee a simple change to a new position.

Besides, issues of safety and cyberattacks are vital in our current reality where information isn't just important yet additionally powerless. Quantum processing, for instance, can possibly break current encryption norms, bringing up issues about how we safeguard touchy data later on.

Exploring the Nexus: Security and Morals in Arising Advances

Exploring the perplexing crossing point of arising innovations, information protection, and morals requires a complex methodology.

Policymakers, industry pioneers, and technologists should cooperate to work out some kind of harmony between mechanical headway and protecting individual privileges and cultural qualities.

One methodology is to carry out powerful guidelines and norms that advance information protection and morals. The European Association's Overall Information Insurance Guideline (GDPR) is an eminent illustration of such guidelines.

GDPR sets severe guidelines for information security, assent, and the option to be neglected. Such measures give people more command over their information and consider associations responsible for how they handle individual data.

Additionally, associations themselves should focus on moral contemplations. Tech organizations can execute moral rules and practices inside their advancement processes.

This incorporates leading moral effect appraisals to distinguish expected predispositions and separation in man-made intelligence frameworks and guaranteeing straightforwardness in information utilization.

Schooling and mindfulness assume an essential part too. People should be educated about their information privileges and the potential moral worries encompassing arising advances. Public mindfulness can drive interest for moral works, empowering organizations and states to stick to better expectations.

The Eventual fate of Arising Advancements, Information Protection, and Morals

As we peer into the future, obviously arising innovations will keep on reshaping our reality. The assembly of man-made intelligence, IoT, blockchain, and different advancements will offer amazing open doors for progress.

Nonetheless, guaranteeing that these innovations are tackled to serve all and don't encroach on security or moral standards is a squeezing challenge.

The excursion forward requires continuous cooperation and flexibility. Moral contemplations should develop as innovation advances, and guidelines should be refreshed to reflect evolving conditions. In doing so, we can expect to partake in the products of advancement while safeguarding the fundamental upsides of protection and morals in our undeniably computerized world.

CONCLUSION

Looking Ahead,Additional Resources Tools and Software for ROI Analysis

Investigating the profit from speculation (return for capital invested) of your substance promoting endeavors is vital for any business hoping to streamline its showcasing methodology. In this steadily developing computerized scene, remaining on the ball is crucial. How about we dig into the apparatuses and programming accessible for return for capital invested examination in happy advertising and investigate the advantages of forward-looking investigation.

Looking Forward: The Significance of return for capital invested Examination in Happy Advertising

As the showcasing scene keeps on advancing, the requirement for return for money invested in happy advertising turns out to be progressively significant. In this day and age, organizations concentrate profoundly on making and dispersing content across different channels, from blog entries and virtual entertainment to video and email promoting. Be that as it may, how can you say whether these endeavors are paying off? The response lies in strong return on initial capital investment examination.

Breaking down the return on initial capital investment of your substance advertising permits you to evaluate the viability of your missions, recognize regions for development, and go with information driven choices. It's not just about making incredible substance; about guaranteeing content adds to your main concern.

Return for capital invested investigation includes estimating the return you get from your substance showcasing ventures contrasted with the expenses in question. This can incorporate following site traffic, lead age, change rates, and at last, income produced. While this idea is surely known, the instruments and programming accessible for such examinations are constantly advancing, offering better approaches to acquire bits of knowledge and go with informed choices.

Extra Assets: Instruments and Programming for return for money invested Examination

Google Examination: Google Investigation is a strong and broadly utilized web examination instrument. It gives fundamental information about site traffic, client conduct, and change rates. By laying out objectives and internet business following, you can straightforwardly gauge the effect of your substance promoting endeavors on your site's exhibition.

HubSpot: HubSpot offers an across the board advertising stage that incorporates instruments for content creation, dispersion, and return for money invested examination. It permits you to follow leads, transformations, and client obtaining costs, giving an all encompassing perspective on your substance showcasing return for money invested.

SEMrush: SEMrush is an extensive Website optimization and content showcasing instrument that gives information on catchphrase rankings, backlinks, and content execution. It assists you with recognizing the best satisfied pieces and upgrading your system likewise.

Ahrefs: Ahrefs is one more vigorous Website optimization apparatus that proposes top to bottom investigation of your substance's exhibition. It permits you to follow natural inquiry traffic, screen contenders, and evaluate the effect of your substance on web crawler rankings.

Buffer: Support is an online entertainment the executives stage that helps you plan and examine web-based entertainment posts. It gives information on commitment, reach, and navigate rates, empowering you to gauge the viability of your web-based entertainment content.

Marketo: Marketo is a promoting mechanization stage that incorporates highlights for lead sustaining and following. It's helpful for B2B organizations hoping to gauge the return for capital invested of their substance regarding lead age and client securing.

Brandwatch: Brandwatch is a social tuning in and examination device that permits you to screen notices of your image and track feelings around your substance. It's especially helpful for surveying brand insight and notoriety.

Tableau: Scene is an information representation and business knowledge instrument that can assist you with making intuitive and shrewd dashboards for content promoting return for capital invested investigation. It's superb for the individuals who favor custom information representation.

Sprout Social: Sprout Social is a web-based entertainment the executives and examination stage that offers itemized investigating your online entertainment execution. It assists you with figuring out the effect of your substance on crowd commitment and development.

Salesforce Advertising Cloud: Salesforce Showcasing Cloud is a thorough client relationship the board (CRM) stage that incorporates devices for email promoting, computerization, and investigation. It's helpful for following the return for money invested in email showcasing efforts and client lifecycle.

The Fate of return for money invested Examination in Happy Advertising

The fate of return for money invested in examination in happy advertising is probably going to be driven by cutting edge investigation and computerization. Here are a few patterns and expectations for what lies ahead:

Man-made reasoning (artificial intelligence) and AI: Artificial intelligence and AI calculations will assume a more critical part in prescient examination.

They will assist organizations with determining return for money invested and recognize content patterns and examples that drive results.

Personalization: Content personalization will turn out to be much more basic. High level instruments will empower organizations to make hyper-designated content and track the return on initial capital investment of customized crusades.

Cross-Channel Attribution: As clients interface with content across different channels and gadgets, cross-channel attribution models will turn out to be more modern. This will permit organizations to grasp the genuine effect of their substance showcasing endeavors.

Ongoing Investigation: Continuous information investigation will turn into the standard. Organizations will require apparatuses that give quick bits of knowledge, permitting them to change their substance advertising systems on the fly.

Blockchain and Information Security: With developing worries about information protection, blockchain innovation might be utilized to guarantee the security and straightforwardness of information utilized in return on initial capital investment examination.

Content Execution Measurements: Conventional measurements like site hits and likes might give way to additional significant measurements, for example, commitment quality, client lifetime worth, and content impact on buying choices.

All in all, looking forward, the eventual fate of return for capital invested examination in happy promotion is promising. By utilizing progressed apparatuses and programming, organizations can acquire further experiences into the effect of their substance endeavors. Whether you're involving Google Examination for web traffic investigation or high level artificial intelligence controlled stages for prescient examination, the key is to remain nimble and adjust to the developing scene of content promoting.

www.ingramcontent.com/pod-product-compliance
Lightning Source LLC
Chambersburg PA
CBHW062332290526
45794CB00005B/2008